BECOMING TITANIUM MAN

Lessons from an athlete and coach who refused to break

The information provided within this book is for general informational purposes only. While the author tries to keep the information up-to-date and correct, there are no representations or warranties, express or implied, about the completeness, accuracy, reliability, suitability, or availability with respect to the information, products, services, or related graphics contained in this book for any purpose. Any use of this information is at your own risk. All opinions expressed in this book are solely the opinion of the author.

ISBN: 978-1-0369-7461-9

Book cover design and layout design by Simon Thompson

Contents

Summary of Major Athletic Achievements

Post-leg break

- Hyrox Asian Open Champion (Men 60–64), Singapore, 2025
- 2nd Place, Hyrox Asian Open Doubles (Men 60–64), Singapore, 2025
- Hyrox Open Doubles Champion (Men 60–64), Auckland, NZ, 2025
- Hyrox Rimini Open Champion (Men 60–64), Rimini, Italy, 2025
- 2nd Place, Triathlon World Championships Standard Distance (Men 60–64 Age Group), Pontevedra, Spain, 2023
- 4th Place, Ironman World Championship (Men 60–64 Age Group), Nice, France, 2023
- Tri NZ National Aquathlon Champion (Men 60–64 Age Group), Taupo, New Zealand, 2023

Seven-time Masters World Champion

- World Masters Games, Sprint Distance Triathlon World Champion (Men 55–59 Age Group), Auckland, NZ, 2017
- World Masters Games, 1,500m Open Water Swimming Champion (Men 55–59 Age Group), Auckland, NZ, 2017
- World Masters Games, 1,500m Track Champion (Men 50–54 Age Group), Torino, Italy, 2013
- Aquathlon World Championships (Men 50–54 Age Group), London, UK, 2013
- Sprint Distance Triathlon World Champion (Men 50–54 Age Group), Auckland, NZ, 2012
- World Aquathlon World Championships (Men 50–54 Age Group), Auckland, NZ, 2012
- World Masters Athletics Championships (Men 40–44 Age Group), 10,000m, Auckland, NZ, 2004

Retired from professional racing in 2004

- Highest ITU Duathlon World Ranking: 2nd, 2003
- Highest world placing: 3rd, ITU Duathlon World Cup Final, 1998
- National Duathlon Champion:
- 2003, 2000, 1998, 1997 (Japan)
- 1991 (Great Britain)
- ITU Asian Cup Triathlon Champion, 1997 (Murakami, Japan), 1995 (Amakusa, Japan)
- Japanese Triathlon Champion: 1993, 1992
- ETU European Duathlon Championships: 2nd (Team UK), 1991
- All-American Athlete, NCAA Cross Country Championships Long Beach City College (USA), 1985
- British Universities 1,500m Track Champion 1983

HUUB
1182
MIKE
HUUB

The Crash

As I lay broken on the side of the road, I had a moment to reflect on the experiences that had left me crippled. My right thigh and hip were throbbing with white-hot pain, possibly the worst I had experienced in my life. I had fallen from my bike during a routine training ride, and the moment my right side hit the ground, I knew this was the kind of injury you don't walk away from. Had I known that morning would be the day my whole life changed, I might have just stayed in bed. But then life teaches us many lessons, and in hindsight, I now believe I am a more understanding, thoughtful, and appreciative person for having gone through this traumatic experience.

That morning, March 2, 2022, I came downstairs after a good breakfast to get ready for a bike ride with my friend and training partner Tim Barnstable. Tim and I were on Ishigaki, a semitropical island in the Sea of Japan close to the shores of Taiwan. We had come down from Tokyo to spend a week focused on our training to prepare for our big races. Tim was preparing for the Cairns Ironman in June. As for me, I had my sights set on the biggest ultradistance triathlon race of them all: Kona.

The Ironman Championships, traditionally held in Kona, Hawaii, is well-known in the triathlon world as the benchmark race for all of multisport. It is considered by many to be the origin of triathlon as it has come to be popularised. Among triathletes, one of the ultimate points of pride is "Kona-Qualified" (KQ) status.

I had spent the better part of the last two years building up my aerobic base, focusing on longer races and even longer training sessions to pursue my goal. I was determined to be the fastest man over sixty on the planet in the three combined disciplines of swimming, biking, and running. My time on the triathlon pro circuit 25 years earlier told me exactly what I needed to do to reach my goal: I had to build the strength and rhythm to push through a 3.8km (2.4-mile) swim, the leg power and efficient body position to maintain the maximum number of watts to push me through 180km (112 miles) of cycling, and the running form and efficiency to kick my legs through a full marathon (42.2km/26.2 miles). My bigger goal at the time was to do all this in under ten hours, a goal that eludes much younger, stronger athletes.

I knew my swim was in order. I had spent at least three hours in the ocean every week even through the COVID lockdowns and just as many hours in pools once they reopened. My son Tommy and my wife Rieko were both excellent and powerful swimmers and had kept me honest with my form. I knew how to rotate my shoulders in the water to minimise drag and propel myself through even choppy seas. I was confident I could be one of the first on the beach. My job for the swim was to make sure I maintained the strength and endurance for the next six months

I felt my bike was also square. I had trained through the brutal Japanese summers, pushing myself on rides hundreds of kilometres long. I worked hill repeats up the peaks of Mt. Tsukuba north of Tokyo and had ridden as far up Mt. Fuji as bicycles were allowed. I could crank on the climbs and spin on the flats. I knew how to hold the aero position for hours, resting on my elbows and watching up the road from just under my eyebrows.

My run was the area where I was most confident. I knew running backward and forward (sometimes quite literally) from my time as a professional and had coached champions for decades. I knew I could carry off a sub-three-hour marathon. Just two weeks earlier when I was tired from my other training, I had done a 30K run in two hours flat.

I had tested all of these disciplines the previous autumn at Ironman Florida 2021. I won my age group in 10 hours and 31 minutes. This earned me the coveted Kona-Qualifier status to take me to the final goal: winning my age group at the Ironman World Championships. If I could get my time under 10 hours, I had a shot at taking a place in history with a world age-group record. To do this, I simply had to knuckle down, do the long, hard sessions, and build on my previous achievements. This is the work of an athlete: take what you've got, and then slowly and scientifically build to the next level. One second faster, one watt more efficiently at a time. I was certain I could get to the top. I was there on Ishigaki to do the work to take home a world championship later in the year and maybe even a world record at the age of 60.

On that day in March, the sky was overcast and threatening rain when we left the rental property on our bikes. We had already hit the beach for a one-hour swim in the ocean, and our training schedule called for a four-hour ride that day. The wind was strong as we set off. I had hoped to get back before the skies opened up as they're wont to do on tropical islands, so I was already feeling a bit uneasy.

To make matters worse, all the peripherals I normally use in my training—my chest-strap heart rate monitor, my power pedals, etc.—weren't connecting properly with the cycling computer I had mounted on my handlebars. Try as I might, I couldn't get it to make a stable connection. It would connect for a second, then I would get a signal beep telling me that the connection had been lost, only to beep at me again several hundred metres later.

As we set off north on the main road out of town, I found myself drifting farther behind Tim as we fought the winds whipping over the farmland that makes up most of the island. My mind wandered to thoughts of my riding position and the minor aches and discomforts I felt on the ride.

I normally tell my athletes on days like this that it's perfectly fine to pack it in and head home. While quantity is important, quality training will always beat a high quantity of garbage training. In retrospect, I should have made my excuses to Tim and headed back or suggested that we change up the plan and do a long run instead of the bike ride. On that day, two feelings were competing within me. One said I needed to push through and make every session work toward getting me to that age-group podium at Kona and verify how my training plan could build a champion, even at my advancing age. The other feeling said that today wasn't going the way

I wanted and that I should just go home and rest up. Moving forward, I now know to respect the voice in my head telling me to call it a day.

As we ventured farther from the city into the farmland, I saw increasing evidence of the cows that they raise on the island. While Ishigaki beef is a delicacy known across Japan, the cow pats they leave on the side of the road were considerably less appetising. In the light drizzle that was now coming down, I found myself getting further distracted trying to avoid these damp, slippery patches on the tarmac and looking around to make sure no two-ton beasts or farm trucks would pull out onto the road. As this was happening, I was falling farther and farther behind Tim, losing him altogether as he rode around bends and over the rolling hills of the island.

To this day, I am uncertain exactly what happened. Perhaps I rode over one of the cow pies that littered the country road. I was still thinking about getting my bike computer to properly connect to my heart rate monitor and pedals, and perhaps I had taken my eyes off the road to look at the screen. Perhaps I hit a patch of wet sand and gravel. Perhaps my tire had a leak and the lack of stability created a wobble. Perhaps a rogue gust of wind hit my wheel at just the wrong moment. Or perhaps it was all of these things creating a perfect storm of bad luck. Whatever the reason, as I came down a small rise determined to try and catch up with my friend, my bike went one way and I went the other. The bike just fell out from under me as I went down hard onto my right leg and hip.

As I hit the ground, I heard a nasty crack and immediately knew that this wasn't just a normal fall. I felt sick, the pain radiating all the way through my entire right side. Something was badly off. To make matters worse, Tim hadn't seen me go down and had kept going down the road out of sight. I was alone, unable to move, with the smell of rain and manure wafting from the fields around me.

The first thing I did was take stock of my situation. I could still move my arms as my thigh and hip had taken almost all of the impact. I was underneath my bike and my shoes had unclipped from the pedals, but the pain in my thigh was excruciating. I had never experienced such pain in my life. Several years prior, I'd had reconstructive surgery on my back, but I could not remember anything that felt as *wrong* as the torment now shooting up and down my leg. I knew I could not move, not even to get out from under my bike.

Tim had fortunately stopped at the intersection at the end of the road and realised that something was off. He soon returned and found me still wrapped around my bike. I told him I couldn't move. He immediately took out his phone and began negotiating with the emergency services call centre. While Tim and I had both lived in Japan for most of our adult lives, as anyone who has dialled emergency services knows, talking with them in the heat of the moment during an accident is actually quite a difficult thing. To then do it in a foreign language is a Herculean struggle. On top of this, trying to give an exact location using verbal directions on a small rural island we had never been to before made things all the worse. I listened in to his conversation as I tried to take my mind off the pain.

Tim: My friend has fallen off his bike. It's a very bad fall, and I think he's broken his leg. We need an ambulance.
Dispatcher: Understood. What's your location?
Tim: Uh... We're on a small road near a farm. There appear to be some sugarcane plants nearby... I can smell cows...
Dispatcher: That could be almost anywhere on the island. Do you know the name of the road?
Tim: Um...no.

Not being a local and not knowing the road numbers, Tim struggled to give the directions. Eventually, patient and professional dispatchers were able to locate us using Tim's cell phone's GPS signal and were finally able to convey my general location to an ambulance. But then we reached a bit of an impasse.

Dispatcher: Okay, I have your location. Please move your friend off the road to wait for the ambulance.
Tim: I'm afraid I can't do that.
Dispatcher: You will need to move off the road. We cannot guarantee your safety if you do not get out of the street.
Tim: I really am unable to move him, and I'm afraid of what will happen if I do.
Dispatcher: Please clear the road.
Tim: I'll do what I can.

Like many other things in Japan, Tim knew that the best way through this situation was to simply say that we would comply but allow our own judgement to decide how to act in the situation. We had fortunately not seen any cars coming down this road the whole time we had been on it. As noted, this was a reason Tim and I had mapped this route. We figured there would be few cars out and about on these narrow paths through the fields, and our prediction on that front held. Besides, any cars coming down the narrow road would hopefully be moving relatively slowly, and so would hopefully see a very tall Westerner standing by his bike, with enough time to stop before running over me and my bright red Ceepo bike. In hindsight, there was so little traffic on this road that I could have been there for hours if I had not had Tim with me. This might have been a very much shorter story. This confirmed what I had known and practised for years: Always ride with at least one other person when riding outside.

Once off the phone with the dispatcher, Tim dug around in the pocket on the back of my jersey to reach my phone. As he pulled it out and passed it to me, my fingers touched the glass and I could feel that it was intact. It was a small miracle it hadn't been damaged, but I was grateful in that moment. The familiar sight of my wife and daughter greeted me

The site of the accident

on my home screen, and their smiles brought me comfort. I knew I had to get home to them. As I thumbed the phone open to call my wife, Tim helped me pull off my helmet to put under my head like a pillow. I hadn't realised how tired my neck had become after supporting the weight at an unnatural angle while lying on my side, but putting my head down granted me another bit of small respite.

I phoned my wife Rieko on FaceTime to let her know what had happened. I told her about the fall, and she was immediately all business. She had been training these past few years as a physiotherapist and acupuncturist, so she knew her way around bodily injuries. Her first concern was whether I'd hit my head—initially, she thought when I called that I might have fallen on my head or neck and that this was a call to say my last goodbyes, as it were. Luckily, I had managed to avoid any head injuries this time, giving her no end of relief. That relief was short-lived as I described the pain in my leg and hip. She confirmed my fear: She was pretty certain I had broken the leg and that I should avoid any movement. The fact that I was still conscious meant that I probably wasn't bleeding out internally, but that all could change with one false move. The artery in the thigh is very close to the femur, and if the femur is broken, it would take very little to sever

the blood vessel. Despite the dispatcher's insistence that I clear the road, it was imperative that I remain as still as possible and stay conscious. While I didn't think I had hit my head, there was still a good chance I might have a concussion. If I started to feel sleepy, it could be a sign of concussion or internal bleeding. Rieko kept me talking and Tim kept me company until the ambulance arrived about forty minutes later. There are forty minutes watching your favourite TV show, or 40 minutes running as hard as you can, and then there are 40 minutes in total agony trying to lie still on a hard wet tarmac road.... Each minute felt like an eternity. Thank goodness for FaceTime! Rieko and Tim truly helped me keep my sanity through the pain.

Once the paramedics arrived, they started the slow process of lifting me safely onto a stretcher. They were very cautious, which is partly why I am still here today to tell the story, but every movement and minor jostle sent waves of agony and nausea shooting through my body. I am not ashamed to admit that it got so bad that I was screaming for them to give me morphine as they loaded me into the ambulance. Fortunately or unfortunately, they weren't allowed to carry or administer strong opioid painkillers. I was just going to have to call on all the reserves of pain tolerance I had developed from my training to get me through.

As they loaded me into the ambulance, I saw a police car pull up. They fortunately saw I was in too much pain to give much testimony regarding what had happened, but Tim kindly answered their questions on my behalf. They gave Tim a card with the location of the main hospital on the island and took off down the road.

The ambulance ride to the hospital was rough and much bumpier than I had felt riding out. Every movement of the vehicle, side to side or up and down, sent a jolt of pain through my body. Rattling on the stretcher, the initial shock of the accident had worn off, but even the smallest jolts amplified the pain a thousand times over. Each small vibration of the ambulance felt like I was being kicked and stomped by a workman in heavy boots.

The agony continued until I reached the hospital. Once I was transferred to a proper bed, I was wheeled into a brand-new emergency room. I was lucky as this hospital had been completed just three years earlier, with a full collection of state-of-the-art MRIs and CT machines and a well-trained staff flown down from the Japanese mainland and Okinawa. Had we been on any other island in this area, the care and treatment I received would not have been as comprehensive. They pushed my gurney into the

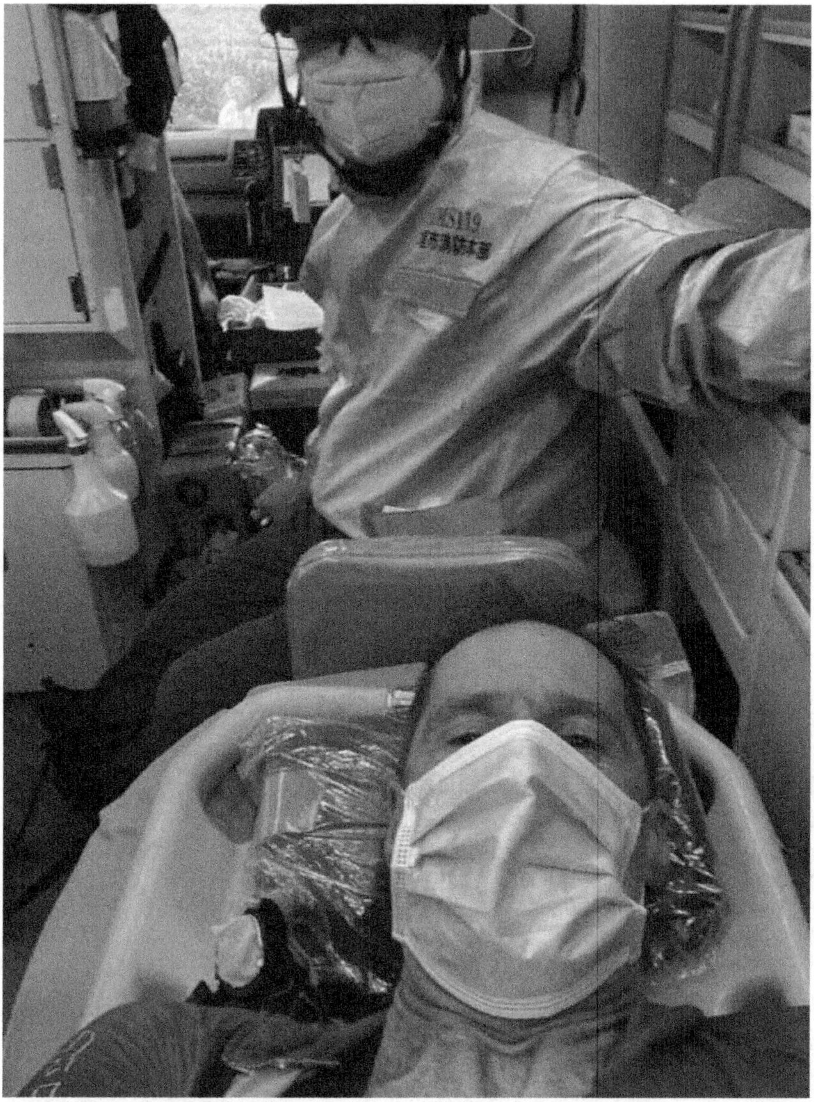

ER, and within minutes a doctor arrived to check me out and begin the tests to find out the extent of the damage.

I had to deal with all of this without any support from Rieko or Tim. Due to the ongoing COVID-19 situation, only patients and staff were allowed in the hospital, and my phone might have interfered with the sensitive medical equipment or been erased by the powerful magnets in the MRI machine. I was truly on my own here, negotiating every instruction to move this way or that in a foreign language.

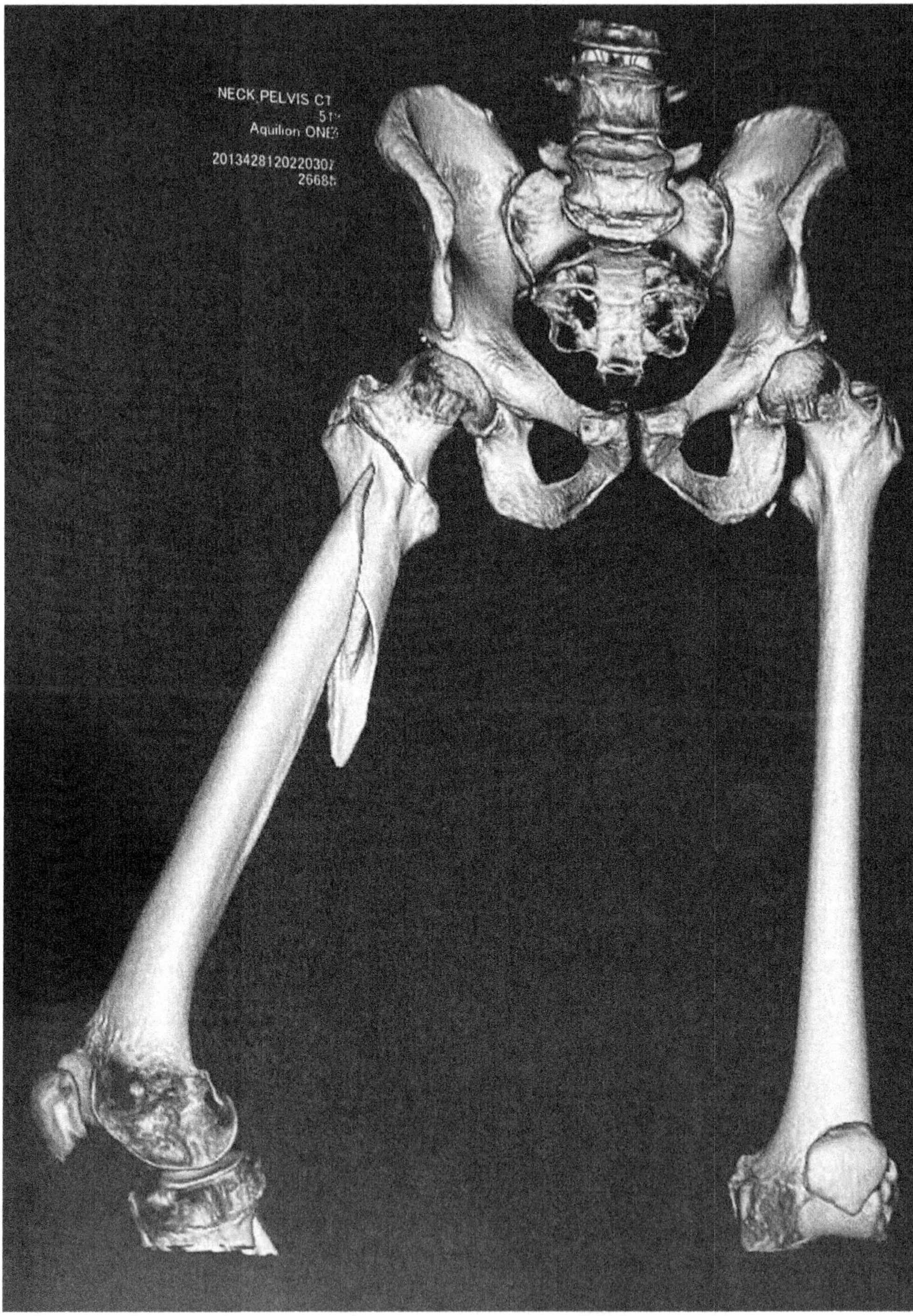

The break

I had thought that once the doctor saw me, I would be given something to help with the pain, but sadly this had to be put off. Pain is information, as they told me, and they needed to know where there was pain in order to get the most accurate images and to make sure they made no mistakes when moving me about. My battered body would have to endure just a bit more abuse, or at least poking and prodding, without anything to relieve my agony.

Lying on the bed as they scanned me, I focused on my breathing—in through the nose, out through the mouth, pull in control, push out the pain. Once the scans were done, the doctors returned to show the images. My pelvis was cracked, and the femur was in multiple pieces. My strong thigh muscles, some of the largest in the body, were no longer properly supported by the corresponding bones. Without the counterbalancing skeletal structure, these muscles started using all the cycling and running power I had developed to pull my now free-floating lower leg up toward my hip, shortening the leg by more than ten centimetres (four inches).

The only silver lining in all of this was that the internal bleeding was relatively minimal. By ignoring the dispatcher and staying as still as possible, I had prevented any further damage. As the scans revealed, the jagged edges of the bones were millimetres from the femoral artery. Had I moved about, those spiked fragments would have punctured one of the largest blood vessels in the body. Worse, an arterial puncture does not clot and would not have stopped the bleeding—even a pinprick can spurt blood at a fantastic rate. A cut in that artery would have filled my leg with all the blood travelling straight from my heart at a rate of one metre (three feet) per second. I would have bled out before Tim had turned around, leaving my cooling corpse on the side of the road for him to discover when he finally realised and turned around. Fortunately for everyone, I had listened to my wife and my gut and stayed as still as possible, preventing an even worse disaster.

Once the hospital staff had assessed the extent of my injuries, it was time to begin the painful process of getting my bones back into place. Out of the MRI room, they let me have my phone again, and I immediately called my wife. It felt good to have a medically trained specialist on my side looking out for me. For Rieko, this was an even more fascinating experience. As an acupuncturist, she was now able to see firsthand the frontline treatment for one of the worst injuries she might have to treat. Her interest in some of the more gruesome aspects of the process at times shifted from a professional curiosity into something almost ghoulish.

"Now, Mr. Trees, we're going to give you a local anaesthetic in your lower leg."

"My lower leg?" I asked, thinking I had misheard. I was fairly confident I knew the different words for the parts of the body in Japanese. "You mean my thigh, not my shin, right?"

"No, your shin. We need to start drilling into the bone."

The realisation of what this meant dawned on Rieko's face as she heard this. "Mike, they have to pull your leg back out. They need to anchor the weights they use into something solid. Flip the camera around so I can see them drilling!" I wish I could say that she looked frightened or worried for me, but her face was lit with fascination at the chance to see this medical procedure.

The attendant came back in with some steel rods and tools that, though pristine and clean, looked disturbingly like they might have come from a local hardware store. The drill itself needed to be cranked by hand! The nurse injected my right shin with the anaesthetic and they went to work drilling the thick pins through my tibia. While I couldn't feel the drill going directly into the shin, the vibration up my leg set off a fresh and unique agony in my thigh.

"Mike! I can't see what they're doing! You have to hold the camera steady!" Rieko's insistence from the other side of the phone brought me back to the moment, and I focused my breathing again. I imagined myself taking catch breaths while swimming, exhaling everything while focusing on catch, pull, glide. I steadied my hand while my wife looked on in fascination at my leg, which was starting to resemble something out of a horror film.

Once they had the anchor points attached, I was ready for the final set of suffering: having my leg pulled back into position. As the weights were attached to the anchor point, I could feel the pieces slowly shifting and lengthening my now-shortened right leg. While I had a local anaesthetic to help with some of the pain, it certainly wasn't perfect, and they hadn't given me anything beyond that. The ordeal was one you couldn't pay me enough to repeat.

Later on, Tim returned to talk to me, and even with the COVID restrictions was able to enter the emergency ward to give me my wallet, charging cable, and a few other necessities he had brought from our rental house. I was informed that Tim would not be allowed back inside the hospital after this. I was fortunate to have a trustworthy friend at that moment. He told me the story of how he had left our bikes stashed behind a concrete shed on the farm right near where I had fallen and ridden back to the house in the police car.

Tim thankfully handled all of the legal concerns and paperwork regarding the accident, though there was one somewhat comical incident he relayed. The police had asked to see both his and my foreign registration IDs for recording purposes. Tim dutifully produced his and then walked over to the kitchen table where I had left mine before we went out for the ride. The police became very tense, ordering him to stop immediately and return the wallet exactly where he had found it. Tim complied and the police relaxed. Apparently, handing over someone else's property could be construed as theft even in this rather innocent (and necessary) situation.

Eventually, my friend had to leave, and this felt something like a heavy door closing. This was the last time I would see in person any friends or family for more than a month. While the emergency ward was somewhat open to visitors due to the nature of the cases they saw, the rest of the hospital had strict quarantine procedures to protect the patients from COVID (and any visitors from catching COVID from the patients in the hospital). In order to receive anything from the outside world, my friend would need to leave the materials at a reception desk and have them delivered to me later.

I was wheeled to the room where I would be staying during my time in this hospital. Eventually, the doctor assigned to my case returned. He would be my surgeon, but he was also the doctor on duty when I arrived—this was a very small hospital! He was young, in his early thirties. Talking to him, I learned he had played rugby at a fairly advanced level. This was lucky as he also seemed to know something about sports injuries and rehabilitation. We began talking that day about my course of treatment and how I was going to get back to competition.

"To fix the leg, we'll have to insert a rod and attach it to the femur."

"Titanium?" I asked, hopefully.

"Yes, that's the plan. We will need to order it from Osaka and unfortunately, we only do these kinds of reconstruction surgeries once a week on this island. Besides, I'm the orthopaedic surgeon, and I'm not ready to take you right now. Most days, I'm back on the mainland. I'm heading back in two days and haven't prepared for your surgery.

The good news is that I'll be back next week, and I'll be fully ready to put you back together. The bad news is you'll have to be in traction until both I and the parts arrive."

A week stuck in a hospital bed didn't sound like much fun. I was so used to being up and about and active, and I didn't even want to think about things like staring at the same four walls and the need to use bedpans. I knew that to get through this experience, I would have to stay positive. Pushing the ideas of isolation, boredom, and humiliation out of my head, I turned toward my rehabilitation.

"Doctor, I've been training for the Ironman World Championships coming up this autumn. I know I probably won't win my division, but do you think I can still go and compete?"

He put down his clipboard and looked at me earnestly. "Mr. Trees, this is a very serious injury. Perhaps one of the worst that can happen without being immediately life-threatening. I suppose it's technically possible your leg will be strong enough to do the race, but you will not have any time to train for it. You'll have to get your fitness back first. More likely, you'll be lucky to be walking without a stick to keep your balance this autumn. Most men your age would hang up their shoes, but I'm sure you'll be ready next year."

At that moment, something shifted in me. I knew I had to prove him wrong. It was the push I needed, and it brought me back to focus. *I'll show you,* I thought. *I'm not most men my age. Not only am I going to be walking on my own, but I am going to be running at Kona in October.*

After the doctor had gone, I buzzed my mate, Tim. He picked up the phone right away.

"I need some weights," I said to him.

"Weights?" he asked.

"Yeah, just something heavy I can use to build the muscles in my arms. I have to stay fit."

"I'll head to the store and see what I can get you."

Tim came through again like a champion. As the sun outside the hospital windows began to go down on one of the most painful days I could remember, I embarked on the long process of building myself back up. On my first day in that hospital bed, unable to move anything but my arms, I started lifting some small dumbbells to prevent muscle wastage.

I had to stay positive; I was here on a beautiful island. My family was safe and healthy, and I had a capable staff to take care of me.

Social media alerts were already coming in through my phone. My friends, clients, and followers were already sending an outpouring of well-wishes and sympathy for my situation. I was going to get back to the top, and the plan for how was forming. Now it was time to create a serious plan and do the work.

Takeaways:

- **Mistakes are inevitable, so embrace them:**
  Accept that mistakes will happen, and view them as opportunities for growth and learning.
- **Prioritise safety and listen to your body:**
  Don't ignore warning signs or push yourself beyond your limits, especially in potentially dangerous situations.
- **Be prepared for the unexpected and have a backup plan:**
  Even with careful planning, things can go wrong, so have contingency plans in place.
- **Cultivate a strong support system:**
  Surround yourself with people who can offer help and support when you need it most.

2

The Long Road Here

There's a special kind of silence that comes after you crash. The kind that swallows sound. A deep, ringing stillness where you can't quite tell if you're breathing, or dead, or somewhere in between. Laid out on the tarmac, with my leg bent in a way it definitely shouldn't be, the hot stench of cow dung wafted from a nearby field, and the crackle of thunder in the humid air signalled an impending storm. The only thing louder than the pain was the thought screaming through my skull:

Not now. Not like this.

But funny things happen when you're forced to lie still. Your mind, suddenly cut free from momentum, starts wandering. And mine did what it always does—it went back. Not to the last race or the accident itself, but further. Back to every scrap, every setback, every time I'd been knocked down and thought, "This is it. I'm done."

And every time, I wasn't.

That broken femur on Ishigaki Island? That was just another chapter. A bloody big one, sure, but not the story. To understand why I knew I'd fight my way back, we've got to rewind. Past the podiums, past the professional races, past the miles and medals. All the way back to a stubborn kid from Darlington who couldn't bloody read.

The Dummies' Class

I wasn't gifted as a kid—not by a long shot. Reading was a proper struggle, a real uphill battle that felt like wading through treacle. My dad, an English lecturer no less, just couldn't understand it. I can still hear his voice, sharp

98

with frustration: "Why can't you just read this, Michael?! You're in the dummies' class! Just bloody read it!" He'd throw his hands up, convinced I was a lost cause and believing that talent was everything.

My mum, though, had a different approach. She believed in putting the hours in. She'd sit beside me for hours, patiently sounding out words, calmly, like each syllable was a small victory. She didn't expect me to be brilliant; she just expected me to try. And I did. Bit by bit, it started to click.

I also found an unlikely mate in Tony Hindle, a whiz at maths and science, but a bit of a duffer when it came to reading, just like me. We ended up in the same remedial group at school. One day, he leaned over, deadpan as ever, and whispered, "You do know this is the class for dummies, right?" That hit me like a slap. I looked around and thought, "Nah, I'm not sticking with this lot for the rest of my life." So we made a pact: we were getting out.

Feeling a bit thick at school, that lit a fire under me. It wasn't until I was about fifteen that the penny really dropped. I stumbled across poetry, and for some reason, memorizing and reciting verses just clicked. It was a strange way into it, but it got me out of those remedial classes. It taught me something vital: if you're willing to slog and show up every day, you can outwork just about anything. Even now, reading isn't my favourite pastime (this is why I needed a co-author to write this book!), but that early struggle taught me that you've got to be a self-starter. That's a lesson that has stuck with me through every race, every injury, and every business venture.

If academics were a fight, I was on the ropes. But sport? That was my swing back. I didn't start as a winner. Far from it. My older sister was the golden child, a natural athlete who won at hockey, swimming, cricket, and rugby. She got bored and moved on. And I, being the scrawny little brother, just followed along. I lost constantly, even arm-wrestling her well into our teens. I was the king of second place, but looking back, that was the best gift anyone could have given me. Losing taught me how to fight.

I started running properly at nine, following my sister to the local running club, Darlington Harriers, one of the oldest running clubs in the world. I wasn't a prodigy, mind. I'd hide in the high jump pit during hard sessions just to avoid the work. But the coaches were good; they let us find our own way. The friendships and the routine cemented it for me. I stayed because of the simple joy of getting a little better each year. That slow climb lit a fire. I started chasing the fast kids, like Kevin Allenby, a natural talent if ever there was one. I never beat him, but I narrowed the gap.

Then came Myles Brown, and his son Mike, one of the top runners in the country. They trained twice a day, and I was doing three sessions a week, mostly getting in their way. One day, they said, "You want to keep up? Then step up."

So I did.

At sixteen, I doubled my sessions. No excuses. Morning runs in freezing wind, evening repeats on empty tracks. That year, I broke through. I was top three in the North East, and by 1983, I even managed to take the top slot at the National University Championships in the 1500m. That's when I realized: talent is nice if you have it, but showing up every damn day? That's the real game changer. And I've been showing up ever since.

While my mates were thinking about jobs after university, I was thinking long. The dream? The Olympics. Not at twenty-one. Not even twenty-five. I wanted the marathon at twenty-eight. That was the plan.

But before that, I needed to see the world. Test myself. So I packed my bags and bought a one-way ticket to the States, setting off on a reckless odyssey that would take me from sleeping on American beaches, to decades later, lying in a Japanese hospital bed with a snapped femur—still asking myself the same question:

How far can I go?

A Young Man's Adventures: From Tunisia to LA

My first proper taste of adventure came early. As a child, my father, an English lecturer, would take a summer job in North Africa teaching English, and we would tag along, exploring the region. Later, when I was sixteen, my sister and I hitchhiked through Europe all the way back to Tunisia. That bug for adventure never left me.

The LA Olympics Journey

It was 1984, and the Olympic flame was burning in Los Angeles. I was twenty-one, fresh out of university, and holding a national university title in the 1500m. But let me be clear, I wasn't invited to the Olympics. I didn't have a coach, a team, or a plan. What I had was a one-way ticket on a budget airline to New York, a massive chip on my shoulder, and a vague idea that I would live in the USA for a year or two.

Spoiler alert: it didn't go exactly to plan.

I hitchhiked west from New York, swapping stories for rides. Along the way, I even met two lecturers who were driving 'drive-away' cars across the country, which gave me a bit of free transport. I occasionally skipped meals to stretch my cash, always telling people, "Yeah, I'm headed to LA for the Games." It made me sound like a contender instead of a chancer. By the time I made it to California, I had about two bucks left, a sunburn that was already peeling in layers, and no place to sleep.

So I slept on the beach.

The first night was alright. But the second and third nights were less

My National Championship Medal for the 1500

romantic—cold, damp, and with no food. I found what I thought was a jackpot: an abandoned trailer with a busted lock tucked behind a petrol station. I slipped inside and curled up on a filthy mattress. I woke up to rats crawling across my chest, and that's when I knew I needed a new plan.

Desperate times call for a bit of creative storytelling. With the Olympics in full swing, I realized my British accent had a certain currency. To the average American, I guess I sounded like James Bond meets Monty Python, so I leaned in, hard! I started telling people I was part of the British Olympic football team. Britain didn't even have a football team at the Olympics, but no one questioned it. I could talk the talk, and my runner's physique did the rest. Suddenly, doors cracked open—free drinks, free burgers, and even a free room for a couple of nights from a charming motel receptionist who thought I looked "important." It wasn't exactly honest, but it kept me alive and fed.

Then, as it so often does in my life, fate walked into a bar one night.

I was sat on a barstool in Long Beach, nursing a warm beer I couldn't afford, when a tall, wiry man with piercing eyes sat down next to me. His name was Deke, a Kenyan track coach at Long Beach City College. He asked what I was doing in the States. I gave him the story that I was an elite British miler out here chasing opportunity—not a lie, but not too far off. A sub-four-minute mile, I said, which was close enough to the truth to feel safe. (I'd run a 3:45.6 /1500m, roughly a 4:03 mile—but who's counting?)

He didn't blink. Just nodded. "We could use someone like you," he said, and offered me a scholarship.

The only hitch was that I'd already used up my university eligibility in Britain. If they found out, I was finished. Deke, and his coach Alice, cooked up a plan: I'd meet Coach Alice in the morning, run a 1,500m, and if I was fast enough, I would probably get offered a scholarship. The following morning, having not trained for six weeks, I ran a solo 1,500m in just under 4 minutes. It was far from my best, but it was just enough to scrape in. All I had to do now was go to the US consulate in Calgary with a letter from Coach Alice. "Don't mention that you've already been to uni," he said flatly. "Let them see what they want to see."

The college paid for a bus journey up north, which was a special kind of hell—forty-plus hours of weird smells, snoring strangers, and meals of vending machine peanuts and tap water. By the time I reached Calgary, I looked like a homeless man who'd been lost in the Rockies for weeks. I walked into the American consulate with Coach Alice's letter in hand and

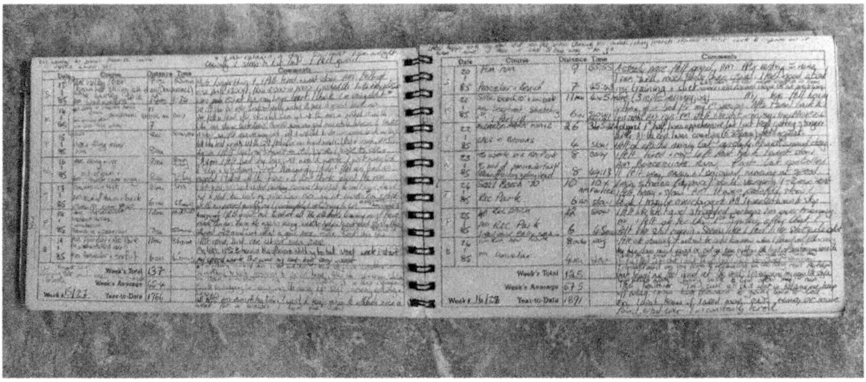

One of my training notebooks from my time at Long Beach

my pulse thumping like a drum solo.

The officer barely looked up. He took the letter, read it, and eyed me again. No questions about my past education. No digging. Just a stamp. Then he said, "Say hello to Coach Alice, I owe him many favours. You're good to go."

And just like that, I had a four-year student visa and a new chance. I stepped outside, grinning like a man who'd just robbed a bank and gotten away with it. In a way, I had. My previous tourist visa had run out, so I had already become an illegal alien. But I sensed life had just turned a corner for the better.

The Knees and the Gun

Back in Long Beach, I threw myself into training like a man possessed. Twice a day, every day. Some weeks I ran 100, even 140 miles. My resting heart rate dropped to 27 bpm, and I built an aerobic engine you could park a bus in. That year, I qualified as an NCAA All-American in cross-country. It was all happening. For a while.

But my biomechanics were a mess. I was overstriding, heel striking, running like a man trying to stamp out ants. My knees started to scream with chondromalacia patella, a condition of worn cartilage behind the kneecaps. Coaches offered cortisone injections to keep me going, but I knew that numbing the pain wasn't healing the problem. The clock was ticking on my legs.

To survive without racing, I took a job at a local motel. Around that time, Long Beach was plagued by 'kneecapping' robberies where owners were shot in the knees if they refused to hand over money. One day, my boss

Running cross-country for Long Beach

handed me a pistol. "If anyone comes in acting funny," he said, "shoot 'em in the knees."

I stared at the gun, then at my own busted knees. It felt like the universe was having a laugh. That night, I lay in bed, knees aching, pistol on the bedside table, and thought, "What the hell am I doing?" It was time to go. I saved up just enough to get back, and headed home.

Finding My Feet in Japan: From PE Teacher to Pro Athlete

Back in the UK in 1985, things were a bit of a mess. I returned home with no job or prospects, with my knees worn down like old tyres, and with a faint aftertaste of America clinging to my clothes. I had put on more than a few pounds being unable to run and subsisting on an American college student's diet. My running career looked like it had been written in pencil and left out in the rain.

I crashed on my sister's sofa, thirty pounds heavier than when I'd left. But my sister, always the practical one, was there for me. She suggested I become a PE teacher, and with the help of her boyfriend who coached me, I went for a postgraduate teaching license at Leeds University in 1985. It felt like a demotion at the time; I still had dreams of racing and glory. But I was broke, and a survivor, so I applied. It turned out to be one of the best decisions I ever made.

I showed up to Leeds out of shape, heavier than I'd ever been, and with knees that still barked every time I climbed stairs. I knew that if I was going to be taken seriously as a PE teacher, I'd need to get back in shape. I went back to basics—cleaning up my eating, cutting out the booze, and focusing on the mechanics. For the first time, I really started studying how to train. I wasn't just a bloke running on fumes anymore. I started understanding form, function, load management, and recovery. I learned how to train **smart**, not just hard. My body responded. The weight came off. The strength came back. And the knees, slowly but surely, stopped screaming.

And just when life was starting to feel too safe, I saw it. A small, barely laminated flyer pinned to the university job board: "Teaching Opportunity: Japan. Seeking adventurous graduates. Apply within." My eyes locked on one word: Japan. I had no connection to the country, didn't speak the language, and couldn't tell you what prefecture Tokyo was in. But something in me leapt. I needed movement. I needed adventure. I needed to run toward something again.

Blagging My Way In

So I applied. At the interview, I found myself in a small, stuffy room filled with intimidatingly polished candidates. Everyone there seemed to speak at least two languages, while I spoke one, barely. So I did what I'd always done: I blagged it. I said I'd spent time in North Africa and was fluent in Arabic—a bit of a stretch, but not a total lie. When they asked me to demonstrate, I rattled off a few phrases I'd picked up in Libya: "How much is this?" and "No, that's too expensive." I guessed correctly that the interviewers would not know any Arabic. A few weeks later, I got the call: I was going to Japan. My best mate, who was a much more qualified candidate, was rejected. Life's funny like that.

I landed in Japan in the autumn of 1986. It was like landing on a different planet. I was sent to teach English at Kwansei Gakuin, a private school with a proud athletic tradition. Although I was hired as a language teacher, the moment they heard about my sports background, they shoved me straight into the athletics department. Suddenly, I wasn't just teaching; I was coaching.

The Triathlon Awakening

Here was the problem: I didn't speak Japanese. And they didn't speak English. Shouting drills across a track using a phrasebook was never going to work. So I did the only thing I could: I trained ***with*** them. Every session, every lap, every rep. I wasn't just their coach—I was their training partner, their pacer, their competition. And that changed everything. They saw me sweating beside them. They saw me limp off the track, then show up again the next morning. Respect was earned, not demanded. Slowly, the barriers dissolved.

The training, too, evolved. I'd damaged my knees badly in the States, and I knew if I wanted a future in sport, I had to run differently. I taught myself forefoot running to reduce the impact. I focused on form, cadence, and posture. My new mantra became: "Practice doesn't make perfect; perfect practice makes permanent." As I started to rebuild, something clicked: I wasn't done as an athlete. Not yet.

Around this time, I started hearing whispers about a new sport catching on in Japan: triathlon. I could run, and I could ride a bike. But swimming? I swam like a stone. Still, the idea of a multi-discipline sport pulled me in. I joined the university swim squad and let them laugh at me for the first few months. I was awful, but I kept showing up. Slowly, inch by painful inch,

I improved. Meanwhile, on the run, I was thrashing everyone. I'd leave the pool red-eyed and coughing, then hammer a 10K and leave half the squad in the dust. It became a game: they taught me to swim, and I taught them how to suffer on the run.

Back to the UK (For Now)

By the time my contract finished in 1988, I knew two things: I wanted to race triathlons professionally, and Japan was somewhere I wanted to build a life. I returned to England to start a Master's degree in Japanese at the University of Sheffield. This was both an academic and strategic decision. I knew that speaking the language properly would unlock the next level for me.

One day, while walking through campus, I spotted a promotional booth for the very same teaching programme that had first sent me to Japan. There, on the banner, was my face! I was now a poster boy for the programme. At the booth, I met one of the original interviewers. "Sir," I said sheepishly, "I've got to admit something. I didn't really speak Arabic." He laughed. "I knew," he said. "But we weren't really looking for linguists. We were looking for survivors who would make the most of the program." He gestured to the poster. "Now we use you to advertise our programme. Who do you think fooled who?"

A Professional Career

By 1991, I was back in Japan. But this time, I wasn't arriving with a suitcase full of lesson plans. I was arriving as something far more dangerous: an athlete with unfinished business. The Master's degree was done. My Japanese had levelled up from survival mode to fluent enough to navigate bureaucracy and banter. I'd been training harder than ever—running with the same ferocity that got me through the worst of Long Beach, swimming like I meant it this time, and learning the intricacies of Japanese culture not just as a visitor, but as a man building a life.

I would be remiss if I did not mention that during this time that I was blessed with my two sons. Akira came along in 1993 and Tomoki (Tommy) was born in 1996. The two boys grew up going back and forth between Japan and the UK following my movements throughout the year, eventually settling in Reading for school. Akira took after my parents, excelling academically and taking top marks during his studies. He is now a gifted photographer. Tommy has followed me in pursuing a more athletic track, training with some of the top runners and triathletes in the world. Both boys, now fully grown, are based in London and excelling in their chosen careers.

Back to the story, the world of Japanese triathlon in the early 90s was exploding. There was money, prestige, sponsorships—everything a hungry athlete could ask for. But it wasn't built for non-Japanese. Foreigners, *gaikokujin,* or sometimes more derogatorily *gaijin* (outsiders) were usually politely tolerated, but not celebrated. It didn't matter how fast you were. If you didn't look or sound the part, you were going to have to fight twice as hard to earn your slot. Which suited me just fine, because I didn't come back to blend in. I came to stand out, to win.

I took the Japanese Long Distance National Triathlon Championship title in 1992 and the standard distance title in 1993. I wasn't supposed to beat local favourites or steal podium spots from athletes raised inside the system, but I did, twice. Sponsors came sniffing, race organisers started putting my face on posters. I did TV appearances and adverts, even ending up on a credit card commercial—me, the same bloke who'd once pretended to be on the non-existent British Olympic football team just to get a burger.

But underneath the medals and media, there was a truth I couldn't ignore. No matter how fast I ran, or how fluent my Japanese got, there was an invisible ceiling. When Olympic selection talk began, I was told—off the record—that the Japanese national team would be made up of athletes of Japanese heritage. Full stop. It didn't matter that I lived there or that I won their races. I was a guest, not a contender. I understood the politics and the culture. If Japan wouldn't open that door, I'd find another.

After years of living and racing in Japan and representing their national team, I returned to the UK in 2004 and pivoted to duathlon—run-bike-run. It was perfect. Even though I was technically a masters athlete at 40 years of age, I was still capable of running under 30 minutes for a 10km. I took my fitness and experience and channelled it into a string of performances that would define the next decade:

- British Duathlon Champion in 1991
- Japanese Duathlon Champion 1997, 1998, 2000, 2003
- ITU World Duathlon ranking number 2 in the world in 2003
- Multiple podium finishes across Europe, Asia, and Oceania

My career culminated in 2004. At the age of forty-one, I qualified for the Olympic Trials in the 10,000m. I knew I wasn't going to win. I also knew I didn't stand a real shot at making the team. But I showed up, lined up against athletes half my age, and gave it everything. I came dead last. But I ran the bloody thing. After decades of injury, rebuilding, political dead ends, and flat-out hustle—I earned that start line.

The Business Years: From Wetsuits to World Rankings

Like most things in my life, I didn't exactly fall into business with a 10-year plan and a pitch deck. It started, as so many things do, with a gap—and a bit of audacity. I was living in the UK full-time, married to Rieko, and racing less but still heavily involved in the endurance community. I knew athletes, I knew gear, and I knew one simple truth: most of the performance products available in Japan and the UK were either overpriced, poorly marketed, or total rubbish. So we started importing a few wetsuits. Just a handful. Quietly. Then a few compression garments and accessories. All high-performance stuff that I used myself and believed in. The orders came in faster than we expected.

Within a year, our little garage-side hustle had outgrown the garage. We moved into a warehouse. Within two years, we had ten employees. Then twenty. Then sixty. At our peak, we had about a hundred staff in two countries, a full logistics chain, marketing, HR, and operations. What started as a side gig became a full-blown machine, generating millions in global turnover.

Let me be honest: without my wife Rieko, it wouldn't have worked. She was the brains behind the operation, sharp with numbers and fearless in negotiation. I was the front man: the athlete, the brand rep, the storyteller. But Rieko? She was the one making sure the lights stayed on. We were an awesome team—married, business partners, co-conspirators in chaos. But it wasn't easy. Building a company from scratch, navigating multiple languages, cultures, and time zones, was one of the hardest things I've ever done. Harder than racing, in many ways. Sport is simple: train hard, race harder, recover. Business? It's never finished. The finish line just keeps moving. But I was addicted to the challenge. The same grit applied. The same stubborn refusal to quit.

While Rieko and I were neck deep in our business venture, our daughter was born in 2010. Amy has followed after her two older brothers, becoming a citizen of the world. She travelled all over with Rieko and me while we were continuing to set up distribution of sporting equipment. She has taken after Rieko, Tommy, and myself as an athlete, though she has chosen to pursue rhythmic gymnastics.

The Northern Echo

Friday, September 29, 1989

The iron man aims to be top triathlete

By NICK HELLIWELL

Michael Trees in training

Cambridge Evening News

DISTRICT EDITION

SATURDAY, SEPTEMBER 16, 1989

Trees hurries in

TWO-WHEEL POWER ... Mike Trees on his bike.

WATER WORK ... Mike Trees, new splash hit.

HENRY COOPER'S KNOCKOUT SPORTING QUIZ

Who...?

Where...?

Clippings from my starting years as a triathlete. Both from September, 1989

Racing Kenny Souza (Left)

Winning the 1992 Kamaishi Hamayuri Triathlon (Right)

新聞　第3種郵便物認可

初のアジア選手権と第6回全日本選手権

内外の"鉄人"800人が挑戦

波崎 トライアスロン

県勢大活躍 団体V2・個人で後藤選手が5位

初のアジアトライアスロン選手権（日本トライアスロン委員会主催、鹿島郡波崎町共催）と第六回全日本トライアスロン選手権（同委主催）が四日、波崎町の新漁港を発着点に開かれ、アジア選手権には中国、香港、インド、韓国、マレーシア、フィリピン、シンガポール、そして国内から約二百人が、全日本選手権には約六百人が参加、体力の限界に挑んだ。全日本選手権では英国人のマイケル・トリーズ選手（稲敷郡阿見町）が大会新記録で優勝した。県勢は後藤文彦選手（勝田市）も五位に入賞し、茨城は団体で昨年に続いて二連覇の活躍ぶりだった。

大会新記録で優勝したマイケル・トリーズ選手＝鹿島郡波崎町の新漁港で

例年よりひと月遅い開催で天候が心配されたが、晴れ上がり絶好のトライアスロン日和。

アジア選手権は、スイム一・五キロ、バイク四十キロ、ランナキロで争われた。日本選手権はスイム二キロ、バイク九十キロ、ラン二十一キロのハーフタイプ。選手たちは海からの強い風に苦しみながら戦った。

給水所は九カ所設けられ、主催者が水、スポーツドリンクとバナナ六千本、レモン千個、スポンジ一万五千個を用意。約千百人のボランティアが手渡しに大活躍した。最高時速六〇キロに達するバイクに、初めはコップを持つ手をこわごわ差し伸べる人が多かったが、波崎高二年の伊藤かおるさん（一七）は「体を引いて手だけ伸ばして渡すのがコツ」と、慣れた様子だった。

全日本選手権で優勝したトリーズ選手は昨年、英語講師として来日した。日本でトライアスロンを始めめきめき頭角を現し、プロに転向したばかり。バイクでトップに立ち、そのまま逃げ切った。「プロになって初めてのレースで、どうしても勝ちたかった。とてもうれしい。風が強くてほかの選手がかわいそう」と余裕の表情を見せていた。

正午にスタートしたアジア選手権は日本勢が圧倒的に優勢。主催者によると、他国はまだ選手層が薄く、バイクも大半は貸しているという。インドから参加したアニュスヤ選手は「風が強くてつらかったけど、レ

全日本選手権の総合二百位までの県内勢の成績は次の通り。

▽優勝 マイケル・トリーズ3時間58分4秒▽5位 後藤文彦4時間10分25秒▽14位 橋本和紀4時間17分33秒▽18位 日笠浩一4時間18分30秒▽21位 寺崎敏彦4時間20分18秒▽41位 中野紗4時間28分38秒▽44位 伊藤慎吾4時間29分59秒▽52位 野口秀光4時間32分28秒▽54位 江藤弘英4時間33分30秒▽73位 野口重勝4時間37分5秒▽85位 佐藤昌一朗4時間39分20秒▽115位 黒沢芳實4時間43分48秒▽116位 中嶋仁4時間44分1秒▽130位 西村世樹4時間45分38秒▽138位 片桐芳男4時間46分59秒▽146位 海老原弘4時間47分33秒▽154位 坂尾米治4時間48分53秒▽165位 深沢美智夫4時間51分3秒▽171位 宮本和美4時間51分31秒▽174位 田畑康之4時間51分47秒▽186位 大竹利雄4時間53分22秒▽189位 長塚孝男4時間53分43秒▽192位 佐伯和哉4時間54分28秒▽194位 平間久夫4時間55分8秒

スストアなどに張ったり、内容を聞く方法で行われ……る税金の項目の意味が分からない」などの相談があった。

常総学院が初V

秋の高校野球県大会 土浦日大と県代表

第四十五回秋季関東高校野球県大会（県高野連主催）は四日、日立市民球場で決勝戦が行われた。夏の甲子園出場校、常総学院が安定した実力を発揮、土浦日大に完封勝ちした。秋の大会での同校の優勝は初めて。両校は三十一日から千葉県で開かれる関東大会に出場する。常総学院は千葉マリンスタジアムで埼玉県の優勝校と、土浦日大は千葉県野球場で神奈川県の優勝校と、それぞれ十一月一日に対戦する。

Report on my first place finish in the October 1992 Inaugural Asia Triathlon Cup

By 2015, we'd been grinding for over a decade. We had built something real, tangible, and profitable. But we were tired—not just the kind of tired that sleep fixes, but deep fatigue. The kind that seeps into your bones and makes you question what the next ten years will look like if you keep pushing. We got a fair, clean offer to sell. It was a chance to step off the treadmill and catch our breath after not having a proper break in over eleven years. So we signed, and just like that, we were out. We walked away with financial freedom, a mountain of experience, and a shared look that said, "What now?"

The Return to Self

With the business sold, I suddenly had something I hadn't had since my twenties: time. Time to think. To rest. To rebuild. We moved back to Japan

Darlington man lifts fourth Japanese title

DARLINGTON'S Mike Trees has become the Japanese National Duathlon Champion for the fourth time.

Trees, who recently scooped the British National title, was as impressive as ever in the Championships, which were held at Wakasaji – a small town by the Japan Sea in the west of the country.

The course was very mountainous, and Trees's gruelling hill climbing training paid dividends.

He was able to control the bike pack to his advantage.

The race over 5km (run), 40km (bike) and 5km (run) was made tougher not only by the long hill climbs but also by the strong winds, but his winter preparation ensured he was in good shape going into these.

In a strong field the run pace was very hot from the gun. Trees was able to drop all but two contenders in the hills during the bike section.

At the start of the second run he pulled clear of these two as well, and won by just under 20 seconds.

The Darlington man is in Japan to improve business links between Europe and the Far East and he spends days studying business practice and the Japanese language.

However, the 39-year-old has still found time to train and continue his successful Duathlon revival.

Owing to work commitments he has not been able to race as much as he would like to this year, but this success puts him in line for the World Championships in the USA in October when, if selected, he will represent England.

On the run: Mike Trees of Darlington on his way to becoming the Japanese National Duathlon Champion for the fourth time

From "The Northern Echo," 12 July 2002

E-mail: localheroes@nne.co.uk SWD **Local Heroes** Friday, April 30, 2004 The Northern Echo 11

Athletics

Cole selected for big race

Middlesbrough AC

Trees takes world title

AFTER a fabulous 2003 for Darlington athlete Mike Trees which culminated in being crowned British Duathlete of the Year, 2004 has begun even better. The 41-year-old has become champion of the world in the World Masters 10K Road Race held recently in Auckland, New Zealand.

In this race the main opposition came from Kerry Rodger of New Zealand who had been fourth in the Commonwealth Games. He set a cracking pace from the start and out of a very large field only Trees was able to go with him.

As Rodger said: "Mike sat on me most of the way then he really hammered the uphill on the second lap."

After the race an elated Trees said: "I badly wanted a world title.

"I have trained hard through the winter for this win. I just hope it has also qualified me for the world duathlon championships next month in Belgium."

Great Britain took second place in the team event, the markers being Mike Trees (1), Steve Murdoch (8), Peter Gray (9).

World class: Mike Trees from Darlington who has won a world title

Swimming

Richmond Dales

Darlington Harriers

Newton Aycliffe

JAMES MOUNTFORD

96.6TFM

Report on my World Championship Title in 2004

for a few years, this time not as business owners or expats on a contract, but as a family, free to live and move at our own pace. I went back to coaching and started training harder again, enjoying the balance of competing and teaching.

I wasn't chasing elite results anymore. I was chasing longevity, trying to prove that a life in sport—when done right—could pay dividends for decades. And it did. After eight years away from consistent training, I made a significant comeback in my fifties, winning multiple Masters World Champion titles in aquathlon and triathlon, including the World Masters Games Sprint Distance Triathlon (M55) and 1,500m Open Water Swimming (M55) in Auckland, NZ, in 2017, and the 1,500m Track (M50) in Italy in 2013. These achievements, alongside my previous British Ironman record, re-established my credibility as an athlete and coach.

All of this set me up to aim for a top spot at the Ironman World Championships. As I headed toward my 60s, I figured I would have a good shot at taking an age-group podium in Kona. I had thought that my background as a professional racer and lifelong athlete would give me an edge, and I was determined to show what I could do. As we saw in the last chapter, life had

other plans, and my road back to the Ironman would require a great deal more twists and turns than I had expected. Turning back to my hospital stay on Ishigaki, I now needed to rebuild and put into practice all the strategies for resilience I had built up over the previous 60 years of sport and life.

Takeaways:

- **Sport is a lifelong pursuit:**
  I have been down and up, but the one thing that I kept doing through it all was sport, and it has paid immense dividends.
- **Consistency is king:**
  Continuously showing up is what brings the results
- **Exercise is always a net positive:**
  In the up and downs, the downs were always worst when I did not have something physical to keep me going.

My view for eight days

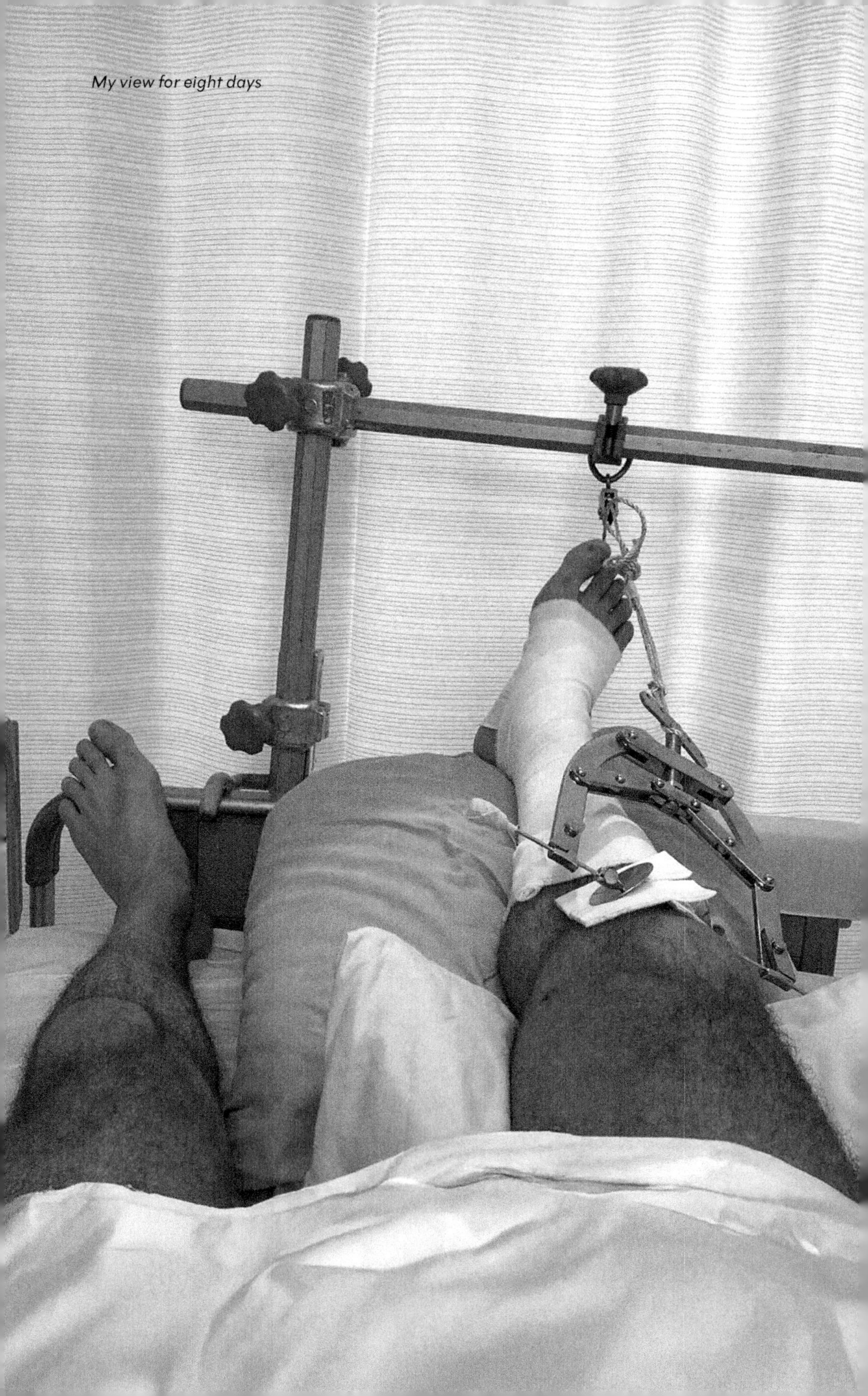

3

Getting Back on Both Feet Literally

I managed to survive eight days in traction, but they were possibly the longest eight days of my life. It never occurred to me how much we move about in a day, but that becomes all the more noticeable when you're unable to. With my leg literally pinned in place and the agony of just shifting weight from one hip to another, there was a fair bit of incentive not to move. Without going into both the smelly and gory details, this week was an exercise in patience and pain management I would not repeat for all the Ironman trophies in the world.

The only exercise I got was lifting the weights that my friend Tim managed to get me. I religiously worked on those every hour that I was awake for a few minutes. Even just a few curls and a few overhead presses kept me sane and gave my mind somewhere to go besides the pain and the waiting. Until this point, I had wondered if there was a limit to how much time I could spend looking at my phone. I can absolutely say that there is. The problem is that when I took a break from screen time, the only thing to look at was a dreary white curtain surrounding my tiny area. As I lifted the weights, I became very familiar with the shapes and patterns on those curtains. I'm fairly confident I could pick out my curtains from a lineup of similarly coloured linens.

I ended up spending most of this time without using painkillers because I wanted to know if I was causing any problems by moving about as I wanted. The traction helped to keep my leg in place, but it was still not held together, and the weight of the traction caused me a lot of pain. I struggled with the nighttime but was blessed to have friends in different time zones all around the world. I would call them during the worst of my sleepless hours, and they would make time to talk and take my mind off the pain.

The worst was that there was this one nurse who was a bit careless. She would bump the weights, causing them to swing every time she walked past. The loss in pressure would cause my muscles to contract, shifting the bones by only micrometres but sending jolts of pain through my whole body. I would shout the whole place down every time she set the weights swinging, and all I would hear was, "Oops, sorry," in Japanese. After the first two times, I thought this was intentional, but the other nurses assured me that she was just a bit clumsy in general. I began to dread her coming around during her shifts. That said, the nurses and assistants overall were amazing and helped me through my recovery, but it goes to show how one person can certainly make life more difficult.

Blinded in Tunisia

Fortunately or unfortunately, my time in the hospital on Ishigaki was not my first time.

When I was sixteen, my older sister and I hitchhiked all the way through Europe. We made our way from France to Tunisia, our first real venture out into the world. We hadn't prepared much, and other than our backpacks, maps, and the clothes on our backs, we were carrying almost nothing. We took the ship to North Africa across the Mediterranean to Tunisia.

Once, following a night out in Tunis, I became ill during the night. Throwing up in the sink of the hostel, my sister found me passed out on the floor of the bathroom.

"Mike, wake up. I think you drank too much."

I blinked but couldn't see a thing.

"Can you turn on the lights, Helen?" "The lights *are* on."

I blinked again, but still no light came in. I reached up and touched my face, but besides the pounding of my headache, I felt nothing. I brushed my forehead, my nose, and my eyes with my hand, but there was nothing blocking my vision.

I felt the cold floor underneath me, tried to push my skinny frame up, and flailed around but slipped back down onto my elbow.

"Uh, Helen, I can't see anything."

"Oh, Mike. We've got to get you home."

Helen helped me stand. She helped me over to the cot I'd been sleeping on, and then I could hear her scrambling about the room. She packed our bags and put my arms through the straps of my backpack before leading me down to the street where we caught a cab to the airport. My sister led me inside the airport, where she sat me down while she spent all but our last 100 dinars on the next flight home. She pushed me through the airport, holding me up by my elbow, and I still couldn't see a thing. Finally, we were stopped and I heard her talking with the customs agent.

"Passports, please. Anything to declare?"

"No, nothing."

"Any dinars?"

"What?"

"Dinars. You cannot take currency out of Tunisia."

"But our flight leaves in twenty minutes!"

"You must exchange them for pounds or francs. No exceptions."

We rushed back through the airport to quickly exchange our currency and then returned to the gate. Helen pushed me out on the tarmac to get on the flight and carried me across the airfield as the sun beat down and the roar of jet engines filled my ears. I could perceive light and darkness, and I knew we were outdoors, but beyond that, I was lost. Without her guidance, I would have run away from the roar of the engines. Thankfully, my sister was a talented athlete as well—she had excelled at everything from tennis to gymnastics with ease in school, and her strength and training paid off that day. She pulled me along at a sprint to the plane with moments to spare. I had barely been lifted onto the plane and dropped into my seat when I heard the jet doors close and the flight staff begin departure preparations.

I ended up spending a week in the hospital upon returning to England. They initially thought I had meningitis but later suspected it was severe food poisoning from eating some undercooked chicken. Thankfully, my vision slowly returned. I never did find out exactly what made me go temporarily blind, and to this day, I avoid most meat whenever I can. For many years, I kept to a fairly strict pescatarian diet.

More than this, I learned how being in hospital feels and what it's like to be completely at the mercy of the body's healing process. I fortunately have mostly recovered, but to this day have small issues with my eyes related to my time in Tunisia.

Blessedly, the eight days passed without other incidents or complications. After the last morning, they wheeled me into surgery where I saw the same doctor who had admitted me.

"Mr. Trees, just try to relax. We have received the proper instruments to put your leg back to the correct length and your feet facing the right way, just like they were before."

"Hold on a moment. You mean there's a chance they'll be different from before?" I felt my heart rate starting to rise.

He laughed. "Maybe if you went to a different hospital, but I would never get it wrong for a fellow sportsman. You'll be walking the same as before in no time."

I relaxed and thought, *No way I'll just be walking the same as before. I plan to be running—and faster if I can!*

Several hours later, I awoke to find the pins removed from my shin and a long line of aching stitches in my thigh. I looked down at my still-numbed leg and was relieved. The doctor had been good for his word; though I could barely twitch the toes, I could see them resting in roughly the same familiar place I had become used to seeing them for the previous fifty-nine years.

As I came to, my surgeon greeted me. "Welcome back, Mr. Trees. It appears the surgery was a success. As you can see, we were able to fit the bones back in almost exactly the same place as they were before the break. Your leg will heal strong and straight."

Still groggy from the anaesthetic, I simply nodded and thanked him. "I would say please be very careful during your rehabilitation, but I know athletes," he gently chided me as he went to leave. "I know you're still going to push yourself, but don't push too hard." A day or two after my surgery, all the damage to my system caused by both the accident and the operation caused my creatine kinase levels to spike through the roof. This put a huge strain on my kidneys. On top of this, I developed anaemia. Both of these relatively minor emergencies required blood transfusions, and I was again thankful to be in a place where I could receive immediate and thorough medical care. The medical team's main priority was to ensure that I didn't die before they could begin rehabilitating me, and their dedication can be seen in the fact that I am still here to tell this story.

After the transfusions, the swelling in my body made me feel like the Michelin Man. Just as before while I was in traction, I was unable to move much and was dependent on nurses and nursing assistants for every basic need. Without going into the details, I really do mean *every* basic need.

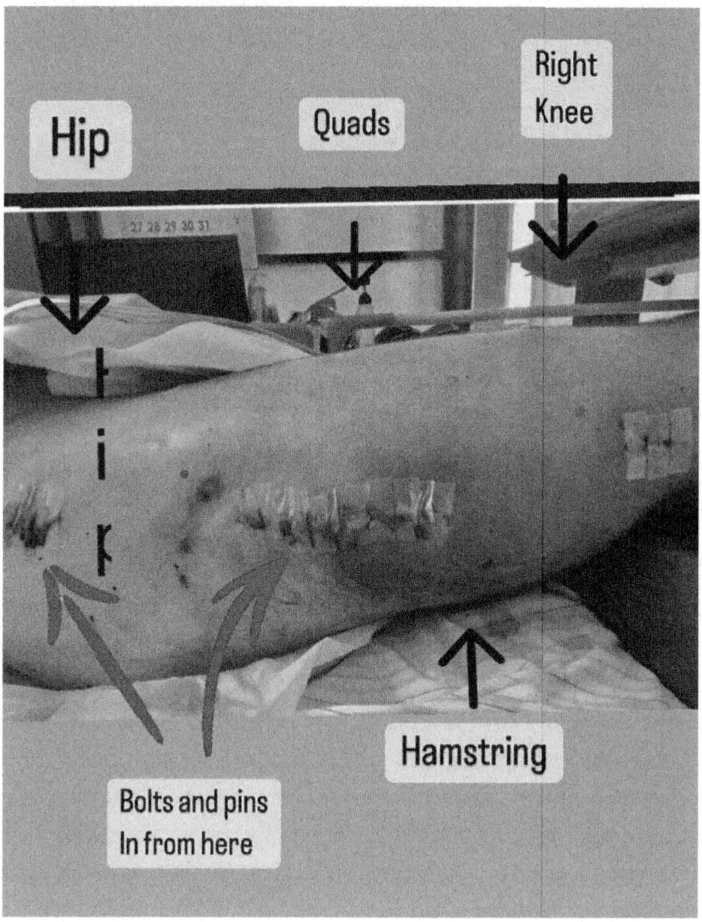

The immediate aftermath of my surgery

Getting out and about at the hospital on Ishigaki

For some reason, the humiliation of being unable to manage fundamental hygiene on my own increased after I came out of traction. After all, I wasn't held in place by weights literally keeping my body in position anymore. I felt like I should have been able to do things on my own now. Sadly, it took a few more days before I got there. I rested, ate, and practised patience. I was grateful to the nurses for their kindness and professionalism—even the one who had bumped my bed so many times!

After the surgical team felt confident my blood toxicity was down and I didn't have any further post-op complications, I was moved to the rehabilitation centre of the hospital. There, I would spend the next few weeks rebuilding my leg muscles. Just as the surgeon had warned me, my proprioceptive muscles were non-existent; my leg just would not work properly. At the same time, I needed to get them back as quickly as possible. Time was ticking down to the starting gun at Kona in October.

One of my first challenges was to use the restroom without the assistance of a nurse. While the nurses so far had been very accommodating, they were perhaps overly so out of a sense of caution. I knew that if I asked for permission to start trying to go on my own, they would say no. So, as the old Nike ad proclaimed, I decided to "just do it." For this, I was chided every time they saw me moving about, but I think they were also glad to have one fewer person to assist with private business.

I decided to time myself to see how long it would take me to get out of bed, into my wheelchair, and across the corridor to the disabled toilet. I called Rieko after my first few trips. "Time me," I told her. "I'm going to the toilet, and I'll call you back when I get back here." Of course, I could time it myself, but I knew that if I had someone watching out for me, and hopefully cheering for me, I'd be all the more focused. As any athlete knows, we can do a private time trial and get a world record when no one's watching, but it won't count until it's repeated and recognized.

The first time, it took me twenty minutes. That put a stake in the sand and gave me something to aim for. I won't say I beat it immediately or every time, but I had something to work on. I thought about ways to make the process quicker and more efficient—where to balance while moving from the bed to the chair, how to place my hands to prevent excess movement and rebalancing, where to put the chair each time so it was easiest to get in. This efficiency training is the kind of thing triathletes know well. We prepare each transition from swim to bike to run, making them as quick and well-organized as possible. By the end of my time in a wheelchair, I was able to do a full round trip in just ten minutes.

During my time in the rehabilitation centre, I worked tirelessly with the physical therapists to regain strength and mobility in my leg. I was still in a lot of pain, and while I had the help of the occasional painkillers, I often did not take my dose. I pushed through it without them to find out exactly when I was overdoing it. Those who do physical endeavours will recognize the phrase "embrace the suck" as popularised by David Goggins. I had to learn how to walk and run again, and I wasn't going to do that by sitting in bed.

The first day we went down to the rehab centre, I started the excruciating process of getting back on both feet. I knew from my training that it was crucial to get the blood flowing, clearing out all the dead and dying cells by getting the heart rate up and delivering fresh oxygen to the wounded area. The problem here was that getting blood flow and movement to that leg was going to hurt nearly as much as breaking the leg the first time.

On the first day, the physio took me out of the bed and tried to bend my knee a bit. At that time, I only had about ten degrees of movement on my own. The muscles in my thigh that had first locked up to try to protect the injury, which then contracted to shorten my leg by ten centimetres, were unwilling to release their hold. The surgeons had further moved those muscles about to insert the rods in my thigh, and the bolts going through the bone were further forcing them to move around in unfamiliar ways. "There's trauma here!" the muscles screamed at me. "We need to stay as taut and firm as possible to protect you!" No matter how much I tried, the muscles would not release and allow me to bend my right knee.

The physio looked at my unbending leg, jutting straight out into space from the wheelchair where I was sitting. He then shrugged and gave me a look over his mask that said, 'I'm sorry to have to do this,' and pinned me down. He used brute force to stretch the contracted muscles that had not been extended in more than a week. I felt like the screaming loser of a professional wrestling or mixed martial arts match, tapping frantically as the physio forced me into submission me by simply bending the leg past forty-five degrees. It struck me in that moment the incredible ways that the mind processes pain. Though I am no stranger to stretching, the pulling sensation of my thigh muscles unclenching was agonising enough to make me forget the pain of the break for just a moment. At that moment, I was strongly regretting my decision to forego the painkillers.

Afterward, he apologised and started pushing my wheelchair back to my sleeping area. I asked if I could push myself. Whether it was out of pure kindness or shame at the pain he had caused me I'm not sure, but he agreed. Wheeling myself about, I began to plot a little course of the ward in the wheelchair. For those next days, I pushed myself around, creating a miniature course I could follow, again trying to figure out the fastest and most efficient route.

One of the most difficult aspects of my rehabilitation was the fact that I was limited to working out in the physio room only in the morning. However, I made the most of this time by doing pull-ups, push-ups, and even racing around the ward in my wheelchair as best I was able. I practised walking using parallel bars and gymnastics equipment and received massages and stretches to help improve my movement. The pain of stretching was nowhere near as bad as it had been that first day and mobility was indeed improving, but I felt like I might progress faster if I had more time on proper rehabilitation equipment.

I would do extra reps getting in and out of my wheelchair or pulling myself to standing on my good leg. I quickly set my sights on being able to walk on my own using crutches. The nurses were hesitant to grant me the crutches so early. It normally would take more than a week after surgery that I would be allowed to use a set of crutches. Fortunately, this was not a hard-and-fast written rule. As anyone in Japan knows, had it been a rule, there would be no discussion. Having seen how I had progressed to independence using the wheelchairs, they agreed to give me early access to the crutches. I worked on finding ways to move that didn't cause as much pain and gradually increased the distance I was able to walk. I started with just going to the restroom and back, then I added a stop at the sitting area at each end of the corridor, where I would sit down, take a break, and then continue on my way.

It was a slow and gruelling process, but I was making progress. I set incremental goals for myself, seeing how many times I could go up and down the hallway without stopping. I started with six trips back and forth, then eight, and eventually ten. I could see the progress I was making, and it really helped motivate me to keep going. Other patients on my ward were amazed at my determination. They asked me how long it had been since my operation and were astounded to hear that answer. I would tell them that I was determined to not let my injury hold me back and that I was going to keep pushing myself.

I decided to take things to the next level and tried taking the stairs to the next floor. In hindsight, knowing what I knew even then about the forces exerted on the body when running down versus uphill, I probably should have gone up the stairs first. Balanced on the crutches, I tried to descend but ended up catching the rubber end of a crutch on the edge of a stair halfway down, and I ended up tumbling all the way to the bottom. I landed with a crack and more pain, worried that I had broken something else. A nurse had seen what happened, and I ended up in the accident and emergency department *again*. They did an x-ray and CT and thankfully everything was still in place, but I was certainly more inclined to take the elevator when going down to the next floor after that. Still, I was glad to know that the pins were holding everything together and my leg was healing properly.

During this time, I was receiving regular CT scans and ultrasounds to ensure that the healing was going apace. For ease of ultrasound administration, the doctors marked my leg where the crack was in my hip and

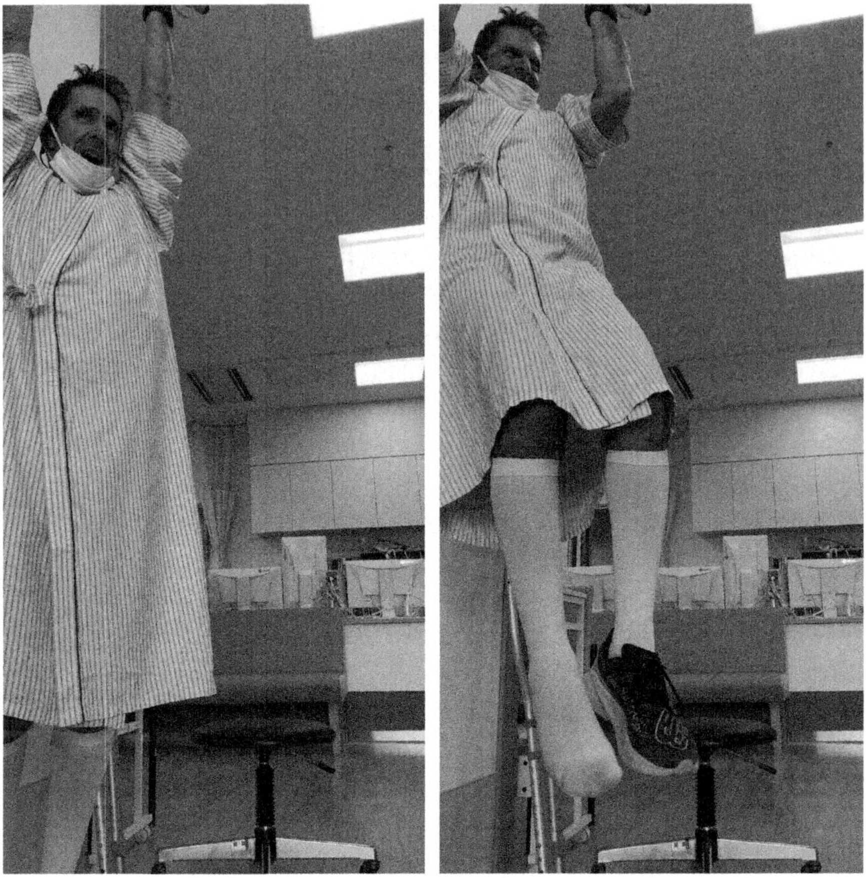

Training my upper body to maintain fitness

pelvis with a black felt-tip marker. One day, I went downstairs for my ultrasound and found that the guide marks had been washed away. It turns out that same nurse that kept banging into my leg every night had accidentally washed away the black markings during my sponge bath! The doctors had no idea where to apply the ultrasound, so I had to go back down for another CT scan to get new markings. After that, nobody touched those markings and I kept a black marker by my bedside. I would reapply the marker to my leg after every time I bathed, a practice I would continue even after I left hospital in order to facilitate my medical care.

I found myself getting into a tedious routine of working out during the day and then waking up in the middle of the night in pain. To pass the time during these sleepless nights, I would often do video calls with friends in California, the UK, or other places around the world who were still awake.

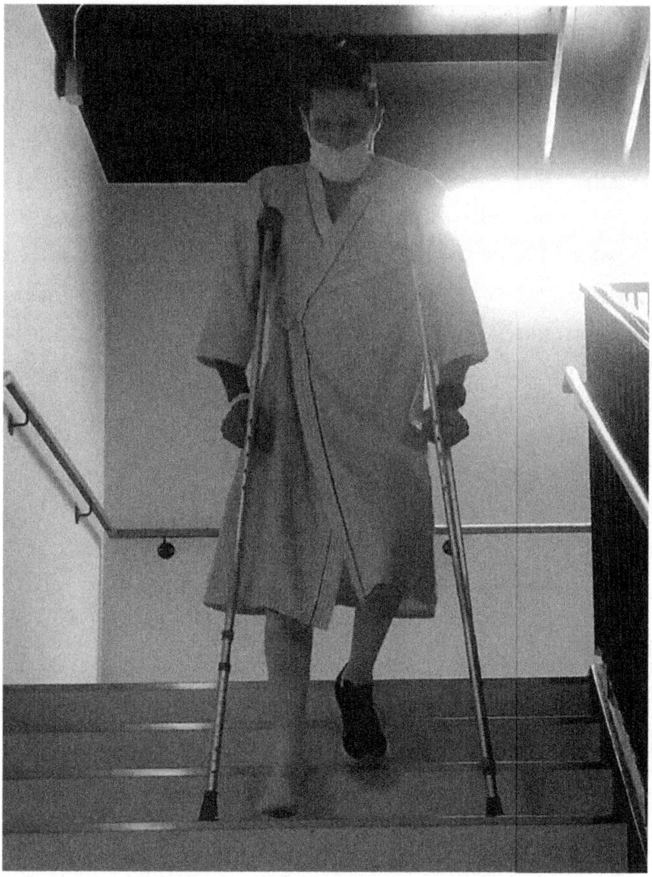

A more successful trip down the stairs

While chatting with them, I would practise standing up, sitting down, and doing push-ups and triceps exercises. I also incorporated plank exercises into my routine, constantly working on building my strength and endurance.

Despite my efforts, my knee would only bend to a maximum of seventy degrees by the time I left hospital. I tried everything I could to push beyond this limit, but it just wouldn't move any further. I was determined to get my knee to bend to at least 100 degrees as this would allow me to ride a bike again. However, it seemed that this goal was out of reach as my knee just wouldn't budge beyond seventy degrees.

The day I left hospital, I was determined to walk on the beach. Rieko had flown down to Ishigaki to help get me back home safely. It was the first time in a month that I had properly been outside, and I just wanted to see the ocean and waves once more on this beautiful island. Rieko kindly helped walk me down to the beach using my crutches. My wife had been training at CrossFit for several years at this point, and I'm truly lucky she is such a strong woman. I was leaning on her most of the way, but she didn't seem bothered by my weight at all. We stood staring out at the sea, looking west into the sunset.

I knew that several thousand miles almost directly west of us was Hawaii. I had my heart set on getting there. Now that I was out of hospital, supported by the woman I love, I was facing the right direction. There was only one straight-line path to Hawaii, to Kona, to becoming more than an Ironman.

Takeaways:

- **Find ways to stay active, even with limited mobility:**
  Even small amounts of exercise, like lifting weights or doing range-of-motion exercises, can help maintain physical and mental well-being during recovery.
- **Set incremental goals and track your progress:**
  Having specific, measurable targets can help you stay motivated and focused on your recovery.
- **Don't be afraid to advocate for yourself:**
  If you feel you are ready for a new challenge or need additional support, communicate your needs to your healthcare team.
- **Focus on efficiency and technique:**
  When relearning basic movements, pay attention to proper form and find ways to conserve energy and minimise pain.

4

Active Recovery

Back in Tokyo, my real training began. The first thing I did as soon as I got back was to schedule a consultation with an old friend from my racing days, my physical therapist Sugiyama Sensei at Takashimadaira Hospital. He had rebuilt me after a previous back surgery, so I trusted that I would be in good hands.

I called him to make an appointment, but all I said was that I had a serious injury. As I hobbled into his office on my crutches, his first question was, "What have you done this time?"

Feeling sheepish, I replied, "I had a bike accident while on a training trip in Ishigaki."

He smiled. "I knew that. The truth is, Rieko was in to see me the week after it happened. She knew you'd be coming here, and we've got a programme set for you." Again, my wife had come through for me.

Sugiyama Sensei had already prepared a set of rehabilitation exercises and sessions just for me. We were going to work on building up the strength, stability, and no small amount of pain tolerance that would be needed for Kona. I would need to turn my legs over for 180km on the bike and then run a marathon, and Dr. Sugiyama knew just how.

"It's a good thing you're a triathlete because swimming is going to be everything you do from now on."

"I was thinking five days a week in the pool," I said cautiously.

"Make it seven. We need to get blood flowing back to the area, and swimming has a nice low impact. You'll be able to move the leg around gently when you kick, and hopefully, eventually do some aqua jogging."

"That sounds great. There's just one more thing."

"New Zealand? Rieko already told me." He was ahead of the game. "Moving house is going to be tough, but so long as you're not carrying any of the boxes around, you should be okay."

Bike injuries: A ticking time bomb

It was 1993, and I was competing in a World Cup triathlon race. We were on Amakusa, Kumamoto, on the southern island of Kyushu in Japan. Back then, triathlon was just starting to gain traction as a sport covered by television. For many of us, it was an exciting time as races were drawing larger audiences and more media attention. However, with that came certain risks that none of us could have foreseen.

During the race, a TV crew was on-site to cover the event, and in the chaos of capturing the action, a cameraman accidentally struck me with his camera as he rolled film from the sidelines in a press vehicle. I crashed on my bike, and the impact caused me to suffer a prolapsed disc in my back. At the time, I was told that this injury would likely lead to problems later in life, but as a competitive athlete, I didn't have the luxury of stepping back. I pushed through, continuing to race and train as best I could. The injury would linger in the background, a ticking time bomb.

Fast-forward to 2015, more than twenty years later, and that old injury finally caught up with me. By that point, my back had deteriorated significantly, and the disc had disintegrated. The pain became unbearable, and I could no longer avoid surgery. It was clear that I needed to address the damage that had been done all those years ago in Amakusa. The surgery was a difficult moment for me, not just physically but mentally, as it forced me to confront my limitations and the long-term effects of my competitive career. I was lucky to have Sugiyama Sensei there to help me run again—his ministrations clearly helped me overcome the problems with both body and mind.

With the luxury of hindsight, we might say now that I should have taken the time to recover properly after the incident in Amakusa. At the same time, I know that if I could go back now, I still probably wouldn't have taken the time away. I knew that I needed to keep racing in those days to maintain my career. The surgery was a major setback, but it also taught me a lot about resilience and adapting to challenges—like the one I faced after my leg break. I learned to balance my rehabilitation with core work and proper conditioning, something I now emphasise heavily when coaching others. It's a reminder that as athletes, we sometimes have to face the consequences of our sport, but those experiences can also shape us in unexpected and valuable ways.

An important twist to the story is that while I was recovering in the hospital on Ishigaki, the immigration service in Auckland had finally gotten back to us. My family was finally given permission to move to New Zealand after five long years of applications and paperwork. The catch was that we had to arrive as soon as possible. The deadline they had set was non-negotiable, and if we did not move right away, our opportunity would be lost and we would have to start over from the beginning.

Rather than throw away all the hard work we had put in securing our move, we decided to push ahead and *just do it.* The timing overall was perfect; my daughter had just finished elementary school and was ready to transition to secondary. Rieko had completed her acupuncture and massage studies, so she was ready to begin the process of setting up a practice. My international coaching business was ready to expand, and I knew several promising young athletes and triathletes in New Zealand who could step up and provide new clients with first-rate training. The only catch was I couldn't lift a box or do any of the paperwork necessary to sell my house.

Without going into the details of the house sale and move, being non-Japanese made much of the work quite difficult. Some of this of course had to do with language, but there were also some inherent small obstacles in the system. Among the tasks we had to negotiate were setting up a listing for the sudden and somewhat unforeseen sale of our condo, ensuring that we got a fair price, and finding a buyer, all while working through the safe social distancing procedures. Fortunately, the work I could do on this front wasn't terribly strenuous. Most of it involved sitting in front of a computer, signing forms at a desk, or keeping the house from becoming a mess when potential buyers were visiting. It was nonetheless stressful, and I would find my leg aching at the end of a day of simply sitting at a realtor's office.

Packing and moving our decade of accumulated goods was a much trickier process. While I could sit on the floor and fold clothing or papers to stack into boxes, I was hopeless much beyond this. As I mentioned, Rieko is a very strong woman, but there were things even she couldn't carry by herself. Several times I called friends to move heavier items to a place where a buyer would pick them up or to my in-laws' place.

The long and short of this interlude is simply to make clear just how much my wife was doing during this time, and I can't emphasise my gratitude to her enough. She literally carried me back from Ishigaki and was figuratively carrying me and my family through this transition to our new life. We have worked through the years to support each other, but during this period she stepped up and saved the day. My recovery would absolutely not have been possible without her, and while this is my story, just as much credit should go to this unsung hero.

Body maintenance

Imagine your body as a complex web where each thread represents a muscle, tendon, or joint. When one thread pulls tight, the tension ripples through the entire network, potentially causing pain and dysfunction in unexpected places. This is the essence of holistic training: understanding how a seemingly isolated issue such as a tight IT band can impact your neck and lower back, how overreliance on forefoot striking can lead to fatigue and Achilles problems, and how heel striking can lead to knee problems.

Mentally breaking free from the 'research paper silo' is key. Don't get caught up in the latest fad or fixate on one specific training style. Instead, embrace the interconnectedness of your body. This means:

- *Address the root cause:* Don't just treat the pain; understand what's causing it. Tight IT band? Look at your posture and strengthen the upper back and thoracic spine.
- *Find your ideal foot strike:* Heel, midfoot, forefoot—the 'best' strike pattern depends on terrain, pace, and even your unique biomechanics. Experiment and find what feels natural and pain-free.

- *Optimize your run cadence:* Aim for a stride rate of around 180 steps per minute. This is best for most runners and can improve efficiency and reduce impact on your joints.

By embracing this holistic approach, you'll:

- *Reduce injury risk:* When your body is balanced and in tune, it's less susceptible to breakdowns.
- *Unlock your full potential:* Optimize your form for maximum efficiency and performance.
- *Enjoy a sustainable running journey:* Listen to your body, respect its interconnectedness, and pave the way for a lifetime of pain-free miles.

Remember, there's no one-size-fits-all approach. Experiment, listen to your body, and seek professional guidance if needed. Embrace any and all advice you that both works for you and allows you to continue every day—then you'll watch your running journey take flight!

Over the next few weeks, Rieko and I worked on the move and spent plenty of time with our daughter, happily liberated from the rigours and strictures of Japanese school before the move to New Zealand. When Rieko and I weren't working or having family time, I was in the pool. I have always been an early riser, but pools in Japan rarely open before nine a.m., and there was little work that could be done preparing for the move besides putting things in boxes. Most days, this left me with four or more hours in the morning to stretch, move around the house on crutches, and work on my core strength. Up with the sun, I would hang from the pull-up bars Rieko and I had installed in the apartment years back, and work on building mobility back into the leg.

Moving about the city, I came to think of getting about on my crutches as another kind of training. I would sometimes use them to do small sets of dips or assist me in doing one-legged squats with my good leg while I was out and about. The crutches and long swimming sets started to enlarge my back and shoulders. My friends and family actually started to notice as my upper body grew broader.

Getting to the large 50-metre pool every day meant leaving the house around eight a.m. Normally, this trip would take me less than thirty-five minutes, but moving there on crutches was always the biggest issue. Fortunately, Tokyo's public transportation is fantastic, and I never had to hobble more than a kilometre from my front door to catch a train, and every train station in the city has ramps, elevators, and other installations to assist people of differing mobilities.

Thanks to my injuries over these many years, I have developed a sense of what differently abled people experience daily. While I will never truly understand the depth of what they go through, I am very sympathetic to their struggles and triumphs. I am likewise quite unsympathetic to anyone who lacks the humanity to assist people in need. Riding the train is one of the places where I noticed most who was able-bodied but still occupied seats intended for those with a greater need. Normally, even though I was on crutches, I did not use these seats. Instead, I used the sway of the train as a chance to work on balance and proprioception. There were days when even I would get exhausted enough to want a seat, and if the car was empty, I would gladly use the priority seats.

On my way to the pool one morning, I noticed an older gentleman leaning unsteadily on a walking stick and very slowly inching his way into the car. All of the priority seats were occupied, and he held onto one of the handholds nearby. I realised then that one had just been taken by a youngish man who started playing a game on his phone. I stood leaning on my crutch in front of his seat and commented loudly in Japanese to the older man, "It's a shame when these seats are full. Are you going far?"

"Not far," he responded. "About six stops." He responded and slowly pointed to the train map on the wall.

I knew this would be about fifteen minutes. While for most people this is not an excessive amount of time, my experiences with my leg had taught me that this could be an eternity if you are experiencing discomfort. This gentleman was clearly much less steady on his feet than even I was.

"Well, I hope someone will be kind enough to give up their seat for you," I responded, again in a theatrically loud voice.

This seemed to wake up the rest of the passengers nearby. The pregnant woman next to the seated young man tapped his arm and pointed to us, me on my crutches and the older man swaying on his cane. Shamefaced, he put away his phone and stood up. The older man gestured for me to sit, but I refused. This man clearly needed to rest more than me, and taking care of those who were in need was taught to me early on as a mark of humanity.

By this measure, the pool staff at the Tokyo Metropolitan Gym were extremely humane. They would always ask if I needed assistance getting in and out of the pool or carefully help me in getting to and around the pool area. I suppose this was done to prevent accidents or other liabilities, but whatever the motivation, I was grateful for the help. While

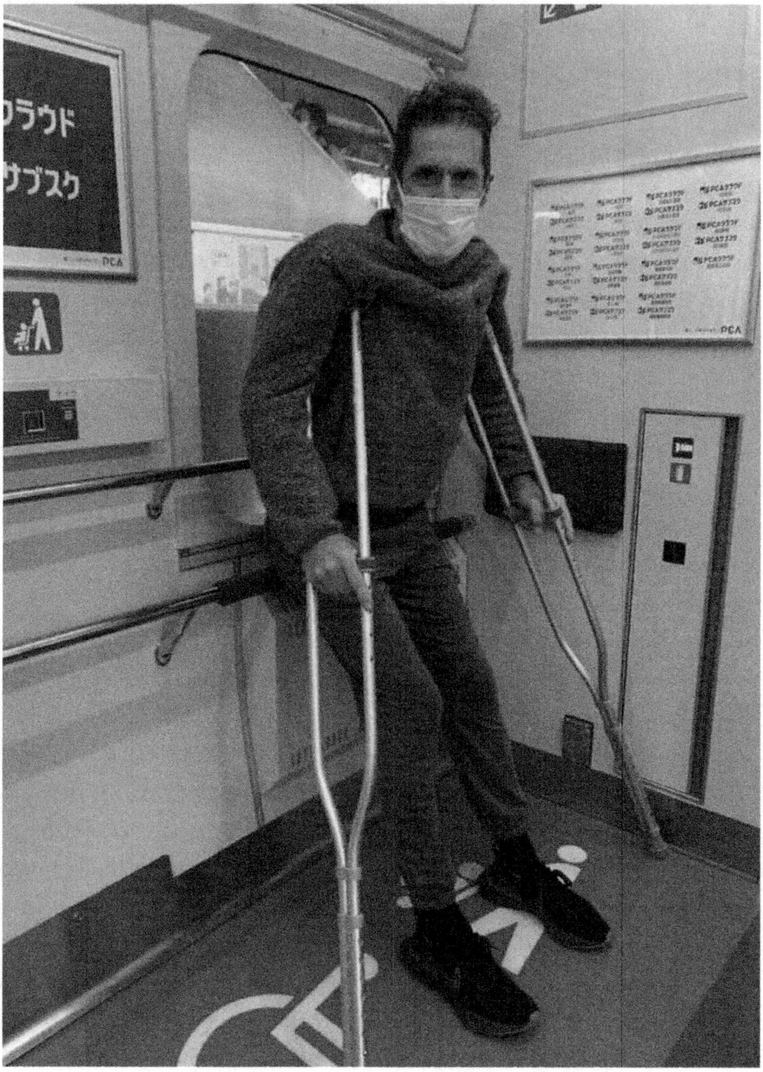

My commutes on the train to the pool

the inane pool rules regarding watches, snorkels, swim paddles, and other training goods normally vex me to no end, during my recovery my goal was not to push out hard sets and measure them well. Instead, I was focused on keeping the oxygen flowing to my injured leg by raising my heart rate, maintaining the fitness I had been building for the past two years. Dryland recovery was helping week by week, but it was definitely not the easiest experience.

Fortunately, once I was in the pool, I found that all of my pain would start to melt away. Most Japanese swimming pools are kept between twenty-five and thirty degrees Celsius (seventy-seven to eighty-six Fahrenheit), which sometimes can feel like swimming in bathwater. When I was doing harder training, I often felt like this was too warm and was always overheating during sets requiring speed or heavy exertion. Not so now. The warm water relaxed my muscles, and floating helped take away much of the stress of recovery and the move to New Zealand.

On a normal day, I would swim for three to five thousand metres and then float over to the aqua jogging lane and do slow walking laps supported by the water; total daily pool time was roughly two hours. In the aqua jogging lane, I could slowly start to push off the damaged leg and again start to build the strength I would need to start running again. The first days of this buildup were painful! Each step put stress on the damaged muscles in my thighs and hips, and moving them through extension and contraction was a struggle. I still did not have full mobility and flexibility, but in the warm water of the pool, I was able to start to build this back up.

The first small breakthrough came in late April, about three weeks after I returned home from hospital. I finally managed to bend my knee past 110 degrees, which allowed me to turn the pedals on my bicycle that was set up on the trainer. On the day I felt like I finally had enough of a bend to my leg, I hobbled my way over to my bike, which would be one of the last things I would pack to ship, and swung my right leg over to put my feet on the pedals and began slowly trying to push. I had to twist my leg a bit to get it to bend. It was agony! Turning the pedals required me to get the leg to 120 degrees, but after a while, I managed to bend it 130 degrees and had a spare 10 degrees in the bend. I had the saddle of the bike set higher than normal to maintain the smallest possible bend in the knee. Even trying to push the pedals around in the easiest gear was brutal.

Road rage and other cycling incidents

Indoor cycling has been a godsent for getting me back into shape, but also in preventing what I am sure would be countless accidents over the years. Cycling can be both exhilarating and dangerous, and my experiences over the years have taught me that no matter how skilled you are, you can never predict the behaviour of others on the road.

One of the scariest examples of this for me came in 1989. I was back in England. I went out for a ride with my friend Kurt Nicoll the former motocross world champion. As Kurt and I were cycling through the town of Saffron Walden, we passed around the side of a parked car. The driver took some sort of offense and honked loudly and repeatedly as we rode away. We made a comment about "all sorts of wankers on the road" but didn't think much of it at the moment. I continued riding in the lead, and a few minutes later, I saw a car coming down this small village lane in the centre of the road. The driver leaned out the window and I just had time to see a meat cleaver in his hand!

Our survival instincts that day were strong, and we were lucky. Kurt and I dove off the road as the car passed, the blade slicing the air where we had been just moments before. Neither of us was injured (and everyone who remembers 1980s steel bikes knows they were impossible to damage), but we were definitely shaken. Saffron Walden was and still is a fairly posh area, and we were fortunate that the homeowner across the street was out polishing his car. He pulled a brick of a mobile phone out of his vehicle, shouting, "I didn't realize how useful this would become when I bought it," and proceeded to call the police. They caught the mad guy with his meat cleaver, but in the end, Kurt decided he didn't want any adverse publicity for motocross, so we decided to let it pass. The lesson remains: There are all sorts of people on the road, and not all of them have our best interests at heart!

Even in a country as safe as Japan, cycling can be perilous. I recall one incident near Mt. Tsukuba, a popular area for cyclists and auto enthusiasts alike, where modified cars race along the skyline roads. The descents are tight hairpins, often fitted with grooved pavement to reduce drifting. I had finished my ride and was descending the mountain at more than 70 kph (~44 mph) when I heard the roar of an over-revved engine behind me. Despite my hugging the side of the road, the driver became aggressive, honking and edging closer with every turn. As he finally overtook me, his car's rear fender clipped my hip, sending me sprawling off the road and over the guardrail. Miraculously, I managed to grab onto the edge of the guardrail, preventing myself from tumbling down the steep cliff. The driver didn't even stop. Though I escaped with road rash and a rideable bike, the experience left me shaken. I'm still haunted by the thought of what could have happened if I hadn't caught myself.

Over the years, I've faced countless other mishaps on the bike. In Tokyo, I was hit by a delivery driver, breaking two ribs. I've dealt with dogs chasing and biting at my ankles, fallen into rice fields due to careless drivers, and even had other riders land on top of me during races and training. There was also the time I jumped a curb on a tough descent and the major crash in Ishigaki. However, these experiences have never deterred me for long from cycling.

The takeaway from all of this is that while cycling is an incredible sport and a massive amount of fun, it is inherently risky. Injuries don't always come from dramatic crashes—there are countless ways to get hurt while riding. My advice? Always ride with others when cycling outdoors. In today's world, especially for those living in busy urban areas, I highly recommend embracing indoor cycling platforms like Zwift. Indoors, you eliminate the risk of crashes, avoid punctures, and have the convenience of food, drink, and toilet breaks whenever you need them. Above all, stay safe out there and keep enjoying the ride—even when it's as painful as the time I was having getting my leg working again.

My daughter, Amy, looked up from her tablet as I started screaming and grunting, but like any teenager, she just rolled her eyes at my struggles and went back to scrolling. Much like the work I was doing in the pool and with my physio, once I slowly got the muscles used to moving this way again, I was able to start to build on success and the pain gradually diminished.

The same week I managed my first painful bike session, I decided to join the weekly parkrun event held near the Tama River on the western side of Tokyo. I have been attending parkrun events for nearly two decades all over the world, and in my more able days, they were often the highlight of my week. Seeing runners of all abilities get together on a Saturday morning to enjoy a good run has always brightened my spirits. I see sport as a social pursuit and love the camaraderie of open events like parkruns.

This week was no different from any other. It was a beautiful sunny day in late April, and numerous friends had come out to support my efforts and see me off. They were all from Namban Rengo, the international running group in Tokyo I have been involved with for nearly three decades, I stood leaning on my crutches at the back of the pack at 7:55 a.m. and waited for the runners to line up. Standing at the back was a new experience. Normally, I'm focused on making this another part of my weekly workout: a speed session where I give it my all and go off to have coffee with friends afterward, achieving the satisfaction of a fast run in the best performance I could do that day. That day, I was simply focused on quietly completing the five-kilometre course as best I was able while limping on my crutches. As a result, I had a chance to line up with friends who I do not normally have the pleasure of seeing at the starting line.

These individuals come to the parkrun each week and work their hardest to run well, get faster, and have a bit of fun while they do it. While they may not break any records, today they would certainly be faster than me! As I stood there talking with them, I realised I was a bit jealous of their ability to run as freely as they did, but I was just as glad to be able to stand with them. Drawing energy from their excitement at the sunny weather and the crowd of supportive friends out for an early morning run, I braced myself to start the race.

As the starting tone went off, everyone took off to run their own race. Several friends started with me but soon realised that I was going to be slow even for them. By this point, I could start to put a bit of pressure on the leg, but supporting the weight of my body was still beyond my ability. I swung on my crutches for the full five kilometres of the course, buoyed by onlookers, friends and family of other runners, and the parkrun race officials. I crossed the finish line with a time of 1:08:41, 52 minutes after the first finisher and a full 17 minutes behind the next person who finished before me, but still not last! While my performance was nothing to write home about, the fact that I had finished a parkrun with a still-healing broken leg left me feeling good.

Completing my first post-accident parkrun

To my knowledge, I am the only person who has completed a parkrun in this exact fashion, though I am certain that there are other stories of triumphs at these events. I hope readers will share some of these so I might highlight them on my social media. Anyone who overcomes adversity to participate in sport deserves recognition, and I am happy to share it when it is due. The people who finished after me also worked at their level, and the beauty of events like this is that everyone gets a chance to participate and do their best.

Another big moment came in early May when I took my first open-water swim with Quint, Tim, and several other friends. It was something of a small reunion for the fateful trip to Ishigaki that began this adventure and the first time I had seen them since my return. Prior to my injury, whenever our schedules would allow, we drove down several times weekly to a lovely beach called Hayama, just south of Yokohama city. This beautiful and serene beach would be the spot for my first post-operation swim—and possibly my last in Japan for quite some time.

More importantly, this would be my first taste of liberation from constantly needing to carefully push off the wall. While swimming in a fifty-metre pool full of bath-like warm water is relaxing, there is something fundamentally different about the open-water experience. Getting out into the ocean is one of the great pleasures of my triathlon training. While I am still not the world's best swimmer, open-water swimming has become a passion for me. This would be a special day and a wonderful sendoff from my trainees and training partners.

The first trial of the day was getting into a wetsuit. Most people who have worn a wetsuit know that putting one on requires a fair bit of wiggling about as well as some careful adjustments to prevent tearing the thick but fragile Neoprene that gives the suit its buoyancy. In this first time putting on a wetsuit since the accident, it really did take all the king's horses and all the king's men to get me in. Though I spent years making and selling wetsuits, I had never considered how a differently abled person might need support in getting into a skintight suit. Tim and Quint helped pull the suit onto my legs while supporting me as I stood, held me up as I pulled the suit over my hips, and then sat me down where I could complete the manoeuvres to push my hands and arms through the sleeves.

Swimming with friends and teammates in Hayama

Afterward, because my crutches were useless on the sand, both of my friends supported me as I hobbled to the water. Once in the water, the suit's buoyancy mitigated any need for help, and I could again feel freedom of movement. The day was beautiful and clear, with no wind or waves, and we could see all the way across Sagami Bay to Mount Fuji. Many people will know the famous Hokusai print, "The Great Wave off Kanagawa." The view of Fuji where we swim is quite similar (thankfully minus the roiling seas of course!). The three of us swam laps of the bay, with Quint and Tim preparing for their next races while I enjoyed the freedom of movement that the water allowed me.

By late May, Rieko and I had concluded the sale of our properties in Japan and finished packing our lives for our new adventure. We flew to New Zealand with our daughter on May 11 and immediately moved into our new, empty home overlooking the ocean. I got a good night's sleep crashed out with my family on mattresses on the floor. The very next day, I went in to see my good friend Matt Brick. Matt is an orthopaedic surgeon in Auckland, but for several years in the 1990s, I was chasing his back tire in duathlons. We had been in touch a bit during the recovery, and I had been giving him updates. I had been walking with only one crutch by the time I arrived in Auckland. As I walked into his office, now only using the crutch for basic support, he gave me a familiar look of both surprise and mild disapproval. "I thought you were spinning a bit of a yarn about how fast you were recovering," he said, "but seeing you mostly off the crutch is a good sign. Still a bit fast, so just don't push it."

I heeded his advice but continued the slow process of getting myself off my crutches. By June, I was making good progress. The next few weeks settled into a fairly smooth routine as I pursued my rehabilitation schedule. I was meeting regularly with Matt and his team in person in Auckland and Donny and Adrian from The Running Room via Zoom and Skype. On top of this, my wife's acupuncture and massage skills were getting daily use in helping me get back on my feet.

In June, I graduated to working on my leg strength from simply trying to build mobility and painless movement. I started doing exercises like leg presses with no weights, trolley pushes, and deadlifts with just a bar. I was also given exercises to complete with elastic bands from my physios in Auckland and a team of friends all over the globe. Bands were great for mixing up the exercises and helping me to continue developing strength and proprioception for other activities, such as running uphill and mounting sets of stairs.

Our first day in New Zealand

One thing anyone who has visited Auckland will know is that it is a city of hills and stairs, and I have started taking advantage of this new obstacle in my training. I started using stairs in my training, first by walking and then by running long sets of stairs whenever I returned from the sea. The run-walk method helped me get up with less shock to my leg. I started by doing ten steps, rest, ten steps, rest. By the start of July, I was able to get up the hill from the ocean without stopping, though the ache in my hip was still a constant reminder of the accident. I found stair training to be a much better workout than running on a treadmill at the gym, as going up reduced the impact through my body quite a lot while also building up the strength in my thigh muscles.

On the beach in New Zealand, my first very painful 10 meter run without crutches

Running drills

Drills for running are a cornerstone of my training as they help break down the running action into its basic elements, allowing me to improve each component before integrating them into a more efficient stride. These drills not only improve running form but also build strength, coordination, and neuromuscular control, which are essential for both beginners and seasoned athletes.

Here are some of my favourite running drills and why I believe they're so effective:

1. High Knees

This drill involves lifting your knees to hip height while maintaining a fast leg turnover. It helps strengthen the hip flexors, improve knee drive, and promote an efficient stride. High knees are excellent for teaching proper posture and engaging your core during the running motion.

2. Butt Kicks

Butt kicks involve flicking your heels up toward your glutes while keeping your knees pointing down. This drill focuses on activating the hamstrings and improving leg recovery. It's also a great way to practise a relaxed, circular leg motion, which is key for efficient running.

3. High knee / Butt kick combo

Bring your heel to your butt as you raise your knee to waist height. This drill combines the previous two drills into a single motion, focusing on the dynamic coordination of raising the leg while simultaneously contracting the hamstring.

Skipping drills

Skipping drills focus on coordination, rhythm, and power. They are excellent for improving both vertical and horizontal propulsion, which are crucial for efficient running. Skipping also helps with neuromuscular development, teaching your muscles to fire in a coordinated sequence

4. B-Skip

B-Skips use forward extension of the leg after the knee drive, which helps improve hamstring flexibility and reinforces the proper leg turnover for running. They require controlled movement and are excellent for practising the pulling motion of the foot back under the body.

5. Standard (High-knee) Skipping

High Knee skipping drills primarily target the hip flexors while also engaging the calves, hamstrings, quads, and glutes. These are performed by lifting the knees to 90 degrees, swinging the arms fast, and focusing on quick leg movements instead of speed over the ground.

6. Ankling

Ankling is a small, quick movement focusing on the ankle's range of motion—you mirror the motions of running but with no knee or hamstring engagement. Instead, bound forward using only the calf and ankle muscles. It helps develop foot strength and teaches runners to land lightly under their centre of mass. Ankling is particularly useful for improving cadence and reinforcing good mechanics at the start of the running stride.

7. Bounding

Bounding is a plyometric drill where you take exaggerated, powerful strides, focusing on pushing off with the back leg and driving the knee forward. It's fantastic for building explosive power, improving stride length, and strengthening the glutes and calves. However, as it's a high-impact drill, I always advise athletes to ease into it gradually and ensure proper form to avoid injury.

8. Pogos

Pogos help to prepare the body for the spring and impact of running. For this drill, jump as high as you can off both feet, using only the calf muscles to push off, then aim to fall on your midfoot, cushioning with the knees. Repeat this motion quickly, minimizing contact time with the ground.

I recommend integrating one to three sets of these drills into a session, combining them with core work and strength exercises. A typical session, including warmup and cooldown, takes about an hour. However, I always caution athletes to approach plyometric drills (such as bounding and skipping) carefully as they come with a higher injury risk. For beginners or those unfamiliar with the movements, I strongly advise seeking guidance from a coach to ensure proper form.

These drills align perfectly with my belief that good running form doesn't come by accident—it's the result of hard work and smart training that targets weaknesses and reinforces strengths. They're an essential part of any programme whether you're recovering from an injury as I was after breaking my femur or training for your next personal best. They provide the foundation for efficient, powerful, and injury-resistant running.

If you'd like to see videos of these drills in action, I've posted examples on my Instagram @run.nrg. I'd encourage anyone to give them a try and see the benefits for themselves!

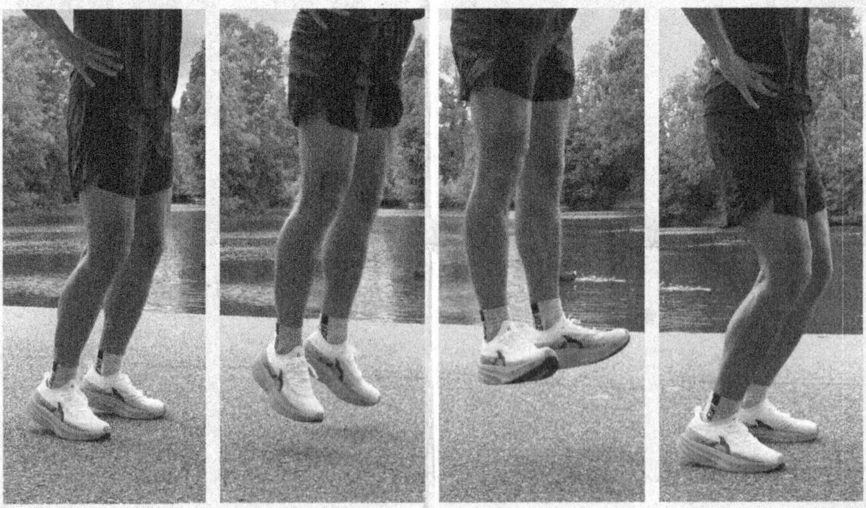

Speed walking at a June parkrun

At this time, I was also able to start basic running drills, again moving uphill to reduce impact. I regularly did butt kicks (or as close to my butt as my right leg would bend), high knees, and ankling. These drills had been my go-to for years when working to build my running-specific strength in the hips, calves, and hamstrings. The fact that I could do many of them now, less than three months after my accident, showed me just how much progress I was making. It was good to finally feel like I was back on track with training, though my running still had a long way to go.

July was a huge set of milestones for me as I finally *ran* my first parkrun. It was an absolute achievement and a proud moment for me, and week after week I was quite literally making bigger strides. On July 16, I was still doing a run-walk at parkrun with a time of 37:24. I had gotten off the crutches at the beginning of June and had started training, but a consistent run was still beyond me at this point. I still lined up at the back of the pack, socializing with the other runners. On July 23, I ran the full course in 27:51, a nearly ten-minute improvement for 5km in one week! Rieko decided not to run and jokingly said, "Now that you're injured, I'll have to start racing you." Little did she know that she'd only have a few more weeks when she could still catch me!

I had decided that I was determined to beat my previous times, and on July 30, I ran the full course in 21:53, which was an absolute quantum leap. The progress continued, and on August 13, I ran the full course in 20:12. By August 20, I improved even more, finishing the course in 19:20. Finally, on August 27, I ran the full course in 18:40, with a pace of 3:44/km (6:01/mile). From walk-running just over a month before to running a fairly respectable time, I felt proud. Being able to do a time like that less than six months after breaking my femur told me that I was ready to buckle down to Kona training. With Kona only three months away, the last months of preparation would be crucial to determine if I'd be able to complete the race. Moving forward was the only way through to the goal, and my family had undergone just as many radical changes as I had. I decided to be strong for them and to demonstrate to the world just what was possible with a goal, a plan, and dedication.

Takeaways:

- **Celebrate incremental progress:**
  Acknowledge and appreciate the small victories and milestones achieved during your training as consistent effort and gradual improvement can lead to significant accomplishments over time.

5

Arrival in Hawaii, 2022

I stepped off the plane in Hawaii four weeks before the World Championships with my friends Stephen Farrell and Niels Madsen. We were there early to ride the course and prepare for the biggest Ironman event worldwide on October 8. Both Steve and Niels had joined me from New Zealand and had been long-term training partners. It was good to be here and preparing for the race with solid training partners I knew I could trust to get me through to the big day.

Steve was a friend from my days as a pro when he was New Zealand's fastest Ironman competitor and has multiple Age Group World Championship titles to his name. He also coached athletes on the New Zealand Olympic team in Tokyo 2021. At that time, I might generously say that he and I were competing in the same age group, but I knew that this time he and I were not even looking at the same race course. Steve would be aiming for a top spot, and for him, this was in reach.

Niels had also been a long-time training partner on my visits to Auckland, aiming for the top of the 65+ age group. He had previously won his age group in several Ironman races across New Zealand and in other spots. He had been training like a demon this past year, so we figured he was a shoe-in for the podium at Kona.

Several days later, we were joined by Alistair Adams, a former Commonwealth Games cyclist. Thirty years back, he had taught me how to cycle properly, while I had helped him get his running in order. He had come to train and settle in like the rest of us and then help me get across the finish line. However, there was a bit of a catch. When we booked the property, we had booked it for five people. However, while five people can indeed sleep in three beds, they have to be quite good friends. The four of us discussed it, and Alastair and I ended up sharing; we're both good enough friends not to have to worry about the awkwardness of two married men sharing an extra-large bed. I figured that as long as I could get to bed early, get my sleep, and get out at dawn, I wasn't going to be fussed about who wanted to sleep next to me. As Ali said, "I don't think I've ever heard myself snore," which was good enough for me not to worry.

Overall, I was happy to be able to bike and run on my own two legs and knew that I would be lucky to complete the course. Being out with these guys I knew I would get great training over the next four weeks.

Unfortunately, getting set up with our rental had been a bit of a nightmare. In and around the date of the Kona Championships, property owners found out it was a seller's market. Ours cancelled on us three time and granted a refund but then relisted the properties for nearly triple the price we had paid. When we complained, they assured us that because we had been fully reimbursed, there was no problem. We begged to differ, having to scramble for a new accommodation that would almost certainly be more expensive given the rising demand. In the end, it turned out to be a much more expensive trip than we had originally expected. Truly frustrating indeed, but there was little to be done. Many of the pros also had the same problems getting there and finding places to train in the run-up to the race. In the end, we gritted our teeth and received assurances in writing that the new owners would honour our original price and agreement.

At the airport, the first fortunate thing for me was having shipped my bike in a simple plastic shipping box rather than a fancy bike case like everyone else. Though there is always a risk in sending my very fancy carbon-fibre Ceepo bike without the added protection afforded by the extra packing and padding of more professional cases, I've learned over the years that a simple box with some bubble wrap is often sufficient to keep my bike safe. More importantly, all I needed to do to pack was remove the handlebars and wheels and wrap the gears and I was good to fly. My arrival in Kona was no different, and after we caught an Uber to our rental property, I was ready to ride in less than twenty minutes.

Once we settled into our rental property, it was time to shake out our

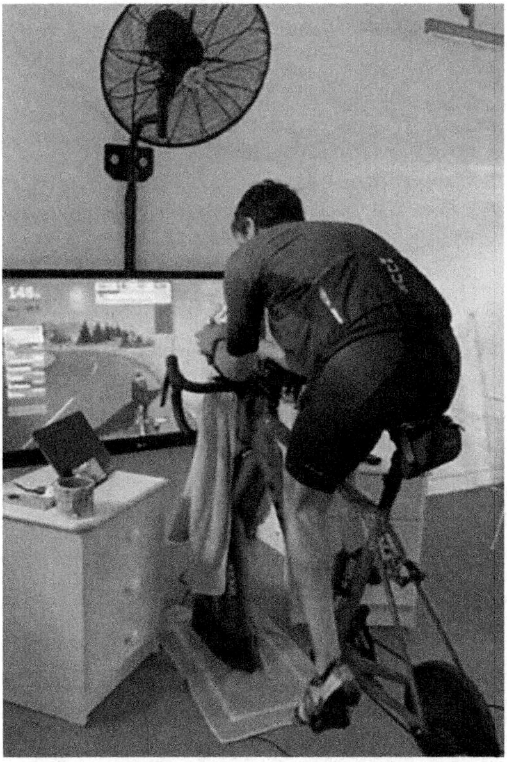

Prior to arriving in Hawaii, I only trained indoors

legs after the long flight. Bikes assembled and unpacked, shoes laid out, and laundry schedules set, we were ready to hit the roads around the west coast of the Big Island. I felt pretty smart having set up my boxed-up bike so easily and was ready to go out for a long easy afternoon ride well before the others. All I needed to do was put on the wheels, remount the handlebars, thread the chain, and pump the tires. I had time to get a coffee and snack before we hit the road, leaning on my bike and relaxing while they were turning wrenches and struggling to fit all of the complicated pieces of their bikes back together.

"Good thing your bike arrived here safely," I joked to Steve.

"Yeah, I'm glad nothing happened to it," he replied.

"Hmm. Yeah, it looks like it's in the same shape as my bike," I said as I patted the saddle. "You think you'll get to ride yours today?" Steve just glared at me as I sipped my coffee.

My comeuppance came as soon as we got out on the road. Either I rolled over something or something happened to my tube during transit, but 200 metres into the first ride on that first day, my front tire went flat. The boys, having not forgotten my jokes while they were assembling their bikes, looked back at me and grinned. One of them said, "I guess we'll see you back at the rental." They took off down the road for a three-hour ride. I pulled off, got out my phone, and fortunately found a bike shop not 400 metres away.

As you can see, it was up and down getting settled in Kona, but fortunately, the rest of the month passed more or less smoothly. We had planned two weeks of hard training, twenty-five to thirty hours a week, followed by a slow two-week taper to get ourselves rested and ready for the event. As I mentioned in the previous chapter, I had still only done a single 30km run before this, so these next two weeks would be the most crucial for building my body back up to the point where I could finish the race.

Each morning, we would rise at dawn to hit the ocean for an hour, aiming to get about three to four kilometres in before breakfast. We could swim every day without too much worry about overdoing it, so we made that a staple of our time around Kona-Kailua. Most days, we would walk down to the beach from the rental, entering with care to protect our feet on the volcanic rocks that line so many of the beaches. From where we were staying, there was no proper beach. It was the place where the lava entered the ocean, and while much of it was smooth, there were definite sharp edges all around.

During one of the more successful rides in Hawaii

As anyone who has been to Hawaii knows, one of the dangers of open-water swimming there is snagging a foot on one of these razor-sharp bits of stone. A nasty cut on my foot or leg would be just enough to tip my recovery away from finishing the race, so I made a point to be extra careful on all the entrances and exits. Entering the water each morning, we had to time it with the waves to make sure we didn't scrape the bottom with our hands, chests, or feet or snag a hand or a swimsuit on any of the rocks. We always had to rely on those same waves to help push us back out again or take our lives into our own hands a bit. It was mostly good fun, and I escaped with some small nicks and cuts on my fingers and toes, but one morning while getting out, I slipped and a rock sliced through my swim trunks. I was fortunate the trunks were big enough to keep me from risking an indecent exposure charge, but after that, I tried to swim when the tide was higher to prevent future incidents and save my swimwear.

One morning, we were passed by a group of other triathletes as we walked across the lava rocks. We recognized a few of them as some of the American athletes, and one called out to us, saying, "Hey, it's pretty dangerous down there. Are you sure you want to swim there?"

Steve shrugged and in his broadest kiwi fashion said, "Sure, if you miss the timing of the waves you'll shave all the hair off your chest, but catch the waves right and you'll be fine." They looked a bit stunned and walked on past toward a more hospitable section of beach.

After the morning swims, we usually had a few different flavours of bike training, mostly designed as stretches of long, low intensity designed to get us used to the heat and tropical humidity of the island. Having just come from the Southern Hemisphere winter in Auckland, we were quite poorly suited to this climate, and there was a necessary period of adjustment. A standard short ride would be two to three hours, while longer days out we'd be in the saddle for four to six hours.

My leg was still in pain, and I could feel the bolts where the rod was still holding my femur together. Though the muscles had indeed healed around the injury and I had regained more or less full use, holding an aero tuck position and pushing into my hips while bent over on the bike for hours at a time would still sometimes give me shocks and cramps at the end of a long day out on the bike.

During the first two weeks of pushing up the endurance, we had planned to ride the full 180km bike course three times just to make sure we knew it as well as we could. The day after Alistar arrived, we went out and I planned to follow Steve and Niels along the course. The problem here was that this would actually be my first outdoor riding since the accident, and I was not ready to keep up with these guys.

With the heat and the wind, I blew up about ninety kilometres (55 miles) into the ride trying to hold thirty-two to thirty-three kph with them. I made the mistake of thinking like my old self, thinking that this was a fairly light pace, but recalled that my plan said for me to be racing at thirty kph so that I wouldn't blow up on the run. I had a small itch in my brain as I was looking at my cycling computer noting the speed but pushed it away, thinking that I could probably hold this speed so long as I didn't have to do any serious running afterward. While thirty-three kph doesn't seem that much faster than thirty kph (*it's only ten percent more,* I'd tell myself), my body definitely felt the increase in effort and watts needed to keep a higher speed over time. Ten percent more speed doesn't translate out to only ten percent more watts. In the end, I couldn't hold my friends' back wheels.

I stopped to refuel a bit at the turnaround point with a coffee and a cold cola to get some caffeine and sugar back in my system, but I was really feeling ill at that point. I just didn't have the strength to keep the legs turning, and my hip was starting to cramp. Niels and Steve were still looking strong, but Alistair and I were a bit green around the gills. After they took off down the road on the return, we turned to each other and I said, "This is just too much." As many have said, practice doesn't make perfect; practice makes permanent. It's good practice that makes you better, and today we were far from good. We both knew that working ourselves into a lather to get back to town would have been counterproductive, building fatigue

Muscular and nervous training

When we train, there are (broadly) two important elements: the muscular system and the nervous system. When we train the muscular system, we are drawing on the muscles' capacity for work at the maximal level, aiming to increase that capacity after they recover. This process is familiar to most athletes. We know what it feels like to train and get stronger. We see greater gains when we use our capacity fully, so we recognize that training ourselves to exhaustion can build up our ability to perform better the next time. This system runs on sugars stored in the muscles and delivered by the blood; the less sugar available to the muscles, the poorer they perform.

The nervous system is more complicated. Nerves send signals back and forth from the brain using a process of electrochemical transfer that uses sodium and potassium. This means that when we are fresh, well-hydrated, and full of electrolytes, our nervous system is working well. Importantly, our nerves remember the way that we contract our muscles: how hard, how fast, how strong. When we are low on electrolytes, the nervous system works less well, but more importantly, it remembers working less well.

In some senses, these two systems are working against each other. While we are depleting our muscles and running them to fatigue, our nervous system is remembering how the muscles contracted and in what pattern, looking for the most efficient way. Once muscles are fatigued, they have less sodium, potassium, and sugar available. While the muscles will build back stronger and more capable of doing work over a long period, the nervous system remembers contracting with less strength because it had fewer resources. When next it is called upon to do work, it will work more like it did when it was fatigued rather than how it did when it was previously fresh. In essence, we have trained our body to work slower because that seems more efficient.

Training when absolutely fatigued means that we might increase our endurance some, but we do so at the cost of overall speed. Our nervous system is now primed to work slower in order to save energy, rather than exert maximal performance because we have taught it that we will probably need to work for a long time.

For a more technical explanation, see the following articles:

Tornero-Aguilera, J. F., Jimenez-Morcillo, J., Rubio-Zarapuz, A., & Clemente-Suárez, V. J. (2022). Central and Peripheral Fatigue in Physical Exercise Explained: A Narrative Review. *International journal of environmental research and public health, 19*(7), 3909. https://doi.org/10.3390/ijerph19073909

Zając, A., Chalimoniuk, M., Maszczyk, A., Gołaś, A., & Lngfort, J. (2015). Central and Peripheral Fatigue During Resistance Exercise—A Critical Review. *Journal of Human Kinetics, 49*, 159–169. https://pmc.ncbi.nlm.nih.gov/articles/PMC4723165/

without creating any fitness benefits or neuromuscular memory. Quite the opposite, we were priming our nerves to move slowly and laggardly by spending hours sweating and exhausted. It was time to call it a day.

About thirty minutes after we lost sight of our friends, Ali and I pulled off the road. We put out our thumbs to hitchhike back to where we were staying. A van driver kindly pulled over and stopped for us and let us out close to town before driving off down the road. When we got out of the van and rode back into town, we found Steve and Niels already back, having finished their ride. "You looked pretty rough out there," said Niels.

"Yeah, we were struggling. It's been tough with my recovery, and Ali's been off the bike for a while."

"Right, well, at least you finished the ride and didn't take the coward's way out, hitchhiking back here."

Ali and I kept our mouths shut and just nodded. We knew we had to keep quiet about this for the time being—I'm sure Steve and Niels will hear about this now that I'm telling the story—but at the time, we really couldn't take the shame. While Ali wasn't going to be racing, I still had a long way to go before I could even hope to finish the course.

I stuck with the boys each day on their rides but knew that there were times I'd need to race my own race, as it were. Much as it stung me not to be able to ride the way I had been just six months before, I kept reminding myself that this was all part of the process of rebuilding myself stronger. I needed to start slower and gradually push up the mileage on these outdoor rides. The next few days were shorter and less ambitious days in the saddle, but we tried the full course again the following week. This time, I was able to hold on for the full 180 kilometres, though we did stop for a coffee and a bite to eat at mid-ride. By the end of the two weeks, I had finally built up my bike fitness to the point where I could complete the ride with minimal stops. I knew then that I could complete the bike section of the race, and with nerves and after a taper, I knew I would be able to at least get to the end on race day.

When it came to the run, this required the most care not in terms of technique and practice but mostly in terms of spacing and load management to prevent injuries or overexertion in the heat. Because repetitive stress of our lower joints would be the most likely cause of an injury, we managed this by switching up the load and focusing on different days. As for the heat exertion, we managed through good hydration and electrolyte consumption.

On one of our first days out on a neighbourhood jog, we luckily came upon a woman putting an old cooler and a set of reusable ice packs by the side of the road. Seeing this, we stopped and talked to her for a moment.

"Are you throwing these out?" I asked her.

"Yeah, just getting rid of them. They're too big and heavy for me to carry down to the beach anymore."

"Is there anything wrong with them?"

"Nah, they just haven't been used in a while."

"Could we take them and wash them out? We're training for the race here in a few weeks."

"Be my guest," she said with a shrug as she walked back to her house.

This turned out to be a lifesaver. We had planned our runs on a 5-kilometre out-and-back course. We could now easily stash the cooler full of ice and cold packs by the side of the road with cold water and colas and have some refreshments to look forward to at each of the turnaround points near our home base. On the long runs, this helped both physically and psychologically knowing that there was a thirst-quencher waiting after every 10 kilometres.

For run training, I scaled back a bit from my previous ramp-up. Having completed a thirty-kilometre (18.6-mile) run just before leaving New Zealand, I had a sense that finishing the run was possible. I pulled back to two half-marathon-length runs the first week in Hawaii. In the second week, I did a thirty-kilometre run at race pace then tapered back down to twenty kilometres (12.4 miles) for my last long run. For each of these runs, I was spending time working out my fluid and fuel intakes, finding the optimal point for getting nutrition, hydration, and electrolytes. With each passing kilometre on these long runs, the heat would wear me down more and more, meaning that I needed to increase both fuel and hydration just to make it back home. Getting these right during the most gruelling portion of the race would mean the difference between finishing and not.

In between long runs, most days my friends and I would get off the bike and lace up our trainers for five to ten kilometres on the road or sand. Running on sand or pebble beaches helped prevent extra wear and tear on the ankles, calves, and knees while letting us build up strength in the glutes and hip flexors to maintain running efficiency. Combined with my focus drills, this helped me keep my legs pumping even after a tough day of working my quads on the bike.

Dynamic Stretches (Pre-run or to wake up and warm up)

These are great to do first thing in the day or before a run. They'll get your blood flowing and prep your muscles for movement:

Single-leg squat

Walking Lunges:

Take long steps forward into a lunge, keeping your back upright and your knee over your ankle. Alternate legs for 8–10 steps per side. This warms up your glutes, quads, and hamstrings.

Calf Raises

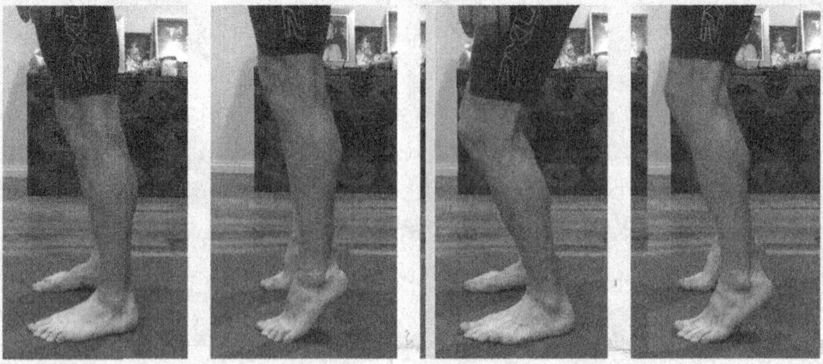

Post-Run Static Stretches (to aid recovery)

Once your muscles are warm after a run, static stretches will help improve flexibility and release tension:

Hamstring Stretch:

Lie on the floor, raise your knee of one leg and put your hands behind the knee. Pull the leg towards your chest with your arms. Extend the lower leg toward the ceiling.

Gluteus Medius Stretch: Lie on your back and pully your thigh across your body. Pull your thigh toward your chest for a deep glute and hip stretch. Hold for 20-30 seconds per side.

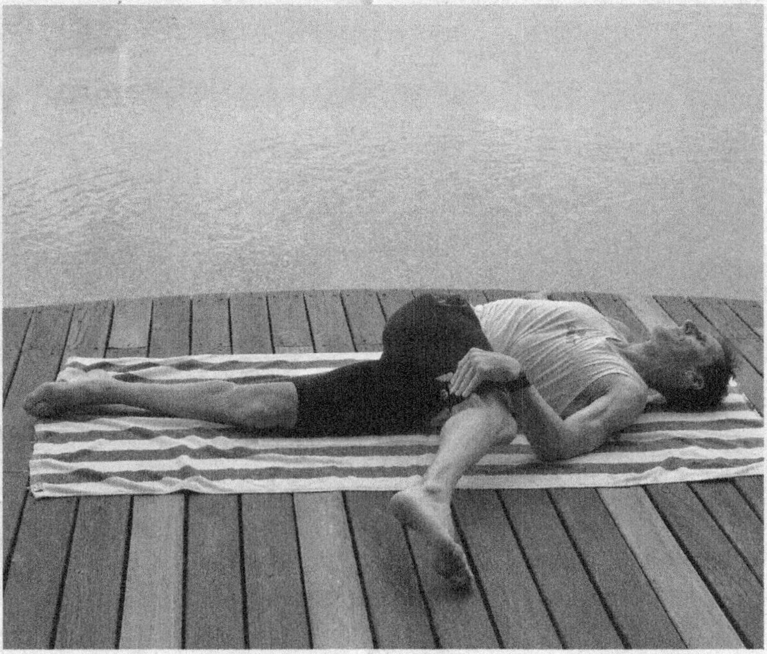

Post-Run Static Stretches (to aid recovery)

Hip Flexor Stretch:

Kneel on one knee with the other foot forward in a lunge position. Push your hips forward gently, feeling the stretch in the hip of the kneeling leg. Hold for 20-30 seconds per side.

Reverse lunge:

Stand facing a wall, place your hands on it, and step one foot back. Keep the back leg straight and the front leg bent, pressing the heel of the back leg into the ground. Hold for 20-30 seconds and switch sides.

Key Points to Remember:

- **Dynamic stretches:** Do before your run or to wake up in the morning. These involve movement and prepare your body for activity
- **Static stretches:** Do after your run or at the end of the day. Only stretch to the point of discomfort, never pain, and hold each stretch for at least 20-30 seconds to get the benefits

As noted in my discussion on rehab in the previous chapters, drills were a crucial element for my run rehab. Finding a short grassy or sandy slope, I maintained the bounding, skipping, ankling, high knees, and butt kicks that had helped me get back to running shape (see "Running Drills" in Chapter 4). At least three times a week, all the way until race day, I would spend at least twenty minutes focusing on every aspect of my run stride in order to keep the strength and mobility I would need for the race. Forty reps of each exercise for six sets seems to be the sweet spot. This doesn't tax my anaerobic system but doesn't leave me feeling underworked by doing too little.

Having done these drills for years now, I knew their basic benefit for my running. Combined with regular foam rolling, stretching, and basic yoga and core work, this strength and conditioning helped me to process the lactic acid that slowly builds over the course of a day of swimming, biking, and running.

More than this, and much more importantly now, I knew in a very real sense that muscular strength was keeping my body from falling apart. At sixty years old, I could feel how every day without stretching, strength, and mobility exercises was a day that my body stopped working quite as well. After that first disaster of a long ride, I got back so exhausted that I basically went straight to bed after grabbing a bit of nutrition and skipped my normal exercises to keep my joints lubricated, as it were. The next day, I found myself moving a little bit less smoothly. After that first reflection, I realised that maintenance is truly an everyday thing even when I'm tired—perhaps especially when I'm tired

I realised that this would be the key difference for me as an athlete recovering from devastating injury. I could be an Ironman made of iron; tough, unyielding, and hard as nails, but brittle. Or, I could be a Titan, made of titanium; robust and able to flex under tremendous pressure, and then spring back to do it again. Drills and mobility were going to be an absolute necessity in order to keep me in Titan shape. I knew that I wanted to be competing and pushing my limits well beyond this race. Though painful and at times boring, I committed myself to being disciplined about drills and recovery in order to make sure I could keep racing even after Kona.

Nutrition was also a major focus of this period leading up to the race. One thing I've been doing for years now as a standard breakfast, race day or any other day, is the banana with peanut butter. This gives me the almost perfect balance of carbs, fats, and protein that I need to get out and do endurance work. The simple carbs from the banana gets me going, and then the fats in the peanut butter help me activate the fat-burning I usually need on long, low-intensity aerobic sets.

One part of the deal we had made was that we would be sharing the responsibilities for cooking. Each of us would switch off each night, and that way we'd be able to make sure we were getting proper race nutrition and plan out what we were putting into our bodies. The problem for me is that while I can assemble a decent meal plan to make sure I get all of my nutrients in, I'm not an expert in making it taste good. To share my end of the load, we agreed that I'd cover dinner out twice a week. Going out to a nice Hawaiian grill or getting something a bit gourmet was also an excellent treat. I planned the training days so that the hardest brick sessions and longest rides fell on my days to "cook." It helped me to finish the workouts on those days knowing that once I had gotten through 100+ kilometres on the bike followed by a painful shuffle in the tropical heat, we could all stretch out on a bench seat at a restaurant, possibly catch a glimpse of some of the triathlon celebrities in town for the race, and just let a professional cover the cooking. It added to the already heavy cost of the stay, but for me it was definitely worth the hit to the wallet to know that my friends would feel taken care of and I wouldn't have to make a mess of the kitchen.

Nutrition Across the Training Cycle

Training Phase • Focus • What to Eat • Tips and Adjustments

Base Phase

Build endurance, recover well. Complex carbs (whole grains, sweet potatoes), lean proteins (chicken, fish, tofu), healthy fats (avocado, nuts), and plenty of fruits and vegetables. Focus on nutrient-dense meals to build a strong foundation. Ensure you're getting enough calories to avoid low energy availability. Timing your meals around workouts is key for recovery.

Build Phase

Increase intensity, fuel harder sessions. More carbohydrates to support higher training loads, such as rice, pasta, and bagels. Maintain lean proteins and add quick-digesting carbs like bananas or energy gels for mid-session fuelling. Pay attention to recovery nutrition. After a hard session, aim for a good mix of carbs and protein within thirty minutes. Keep hydration in check with electrolytes.

Taper Phase

Reduce training load, store glycogen for race day. Carb-loading becomes essential—think white rice, pasta, and low-fibre options. Keep meals simple, and avoid foods and beverages that might upset your stomach. Avoid trying anything new at this stage. Stick to foods you know work for you. Reduce fibre intake to prevent gastrointestinal issues on race day.

Foods to Eat and Avoid on Race Day

Race-day nutrition is all about simplicity and reliability. The last thing you want is to sabotage all your hard work by eating the wrong thing or timing your meals poorly. Here's what I've learned from years of experience:

Foods to Eat

- *Breakfast:* My go-to pre-race breakfast is two white bagel halves with strawberry jam and a cup of coffee. It's light, easy to digest, and provides a good hit of carbs to top up glycogen stores. This is usually eaten three to four hours before the race starts.
- *During the Race:* Stick to what you've practised in training. For me, that means energy gels, electrolyte drinks, and sometimes bananas if I'm on the bike leg of a triathlon. The key is to keep fuelling regularly—don't wait until you feel tired or hungry.
- *Hydration:* Electrolyte drinks are essential, especially for longer races. They help replace lost salts and keep your energy levels stable. Make sure you've practised drinking during training so your stomach is used to it.

Foods to Avoid

- *High-Fibre Foods:* While fibre is great for general health, it's the last thing you want on race day. Avoid whole grains, beans, and anything else that might upset your stomach—or worse, send you searching for the porta-loo in the middle of the race.
- *Heavy Fats and Proteins:* Skip greasy breakfasts or anything too rich as these can slow digestion and leave you feeling lethargic.
- *Unfamiliar Foods:* Race day is not the time to experiment. Stick to what you know works for your body. If you're racing abroad, plan ahead and pack your own fuel if possible.

The final piece of the puzzle was the brick workouts—bike workouts followed by runs. I had calculated that we would need two bricks during the buildup phase, which always took the form of a ninety-kilometre bike ride near the course followed by a ninety-minute run. This was to make sure I could run off the bike. With the move to New Zealand, the focus on recovery, and the need to get back on my feet, I had done no brick work at all before going to Hawaii.

Most racers and professional coaches coming into this would look at my training plan and say, "Well, that's ridiculous. You can't do an Ironman on three brick sessions." For most people, this is true, but we are also the sum total of what got us here. My experience prior to the accident gave me an advantage here. I just needed to remind myself and reassure myself that I could still run off the bike. Those two sessions did it. I was able to finish the ninety-kilometre ride and then run continuously for ninety minutes without stopping or walking. The first brick session showed me it was possible, while the second session showed that the first one wasn't a fluke. This gave me the confidence going into the taper period that I had the fitness required to finish the race.

Week	Day	Workout	Description	Effort
1	Monday	Off	Bike or Swim Focus Day	-
	Tuesday	Intervals	8 x 800m at 5K pace, 90-second jog recovery	8
	Wednesday	Easy Run	45 minutes easy, focus on recovery	4
	Thursday	Off	Swim Focus Day	-
	Friday	Tempo Run	20-minute warmup, 30 minutes at half-marathon pace, 10-minute cooldown	7
	Saturday	Long Run	90 minutes easy with 4 x 5-minute surges at 10K pace near the end (2-minute recovery)	6-7
	Sunday	Off	Bike Focus Day	-

2	Monday	Off	Swim or Bike Focus Day	-
	Tuesday	Hill Repeats	10 x 45-second uphill sprints, jog back recovery	8
	Wednesday	Easy Run	50 minutes easy, focus on recovery	4
	Thursday	Off	Bike Focus Day	-
	Friday	Progression Run	10-minute warmup, 40 minutes progressing from easy to 10K pace, 10-minute cooldown	6-8
	Saturday	Long Run	100 minutes steady, 10 minutes at marathon pace toward the end	6-7
	Sunday	Off	Swim Focus Day	-
3	Monday	Off	Bike or Swim Focus Day	-
	Tuesday	Intervals	6 x 1-mile at 10K pace, 2-minute jog recovery	8
	Wednesday	Easy Run	45 minutes recovery pace	4
	Thursday	Off	Bike Focus Day	-
	Friday	Tempo Run	15-minute warmup, 3 x 10 minutes at half-marathon pace with 5-minute recovery jog, 10-minute cooldown	7
	Saturday	Long Run	110 minutes easy with strides (8 x 20 seconds at 5K pace) in the final 20 minutes	6-7
	Sunday	Off	Swim Focus Day	-
4	Monday	Off	Swim or Bike Focus Day	-
	Tuesday	Intervals	10 x 400m at 3K pace, 90-second jog recovery	9
	Wednesday	Easy Run	40 minutes very easy, focus on recovery	3-4
	Thursday	Off	Bike Focus Day	-

4	Friday	Tempo Run	20-minute warmup, 40 minutes at half-marathon pace, 10-minute cooldown	7
	Saturday	Long Run	120 minutes steady, last 20 minutes at marathon pace	6-7
	Sunday	Off	Swim Focus Day	-
5	Monday	Off	Bike or Swim Focus Day	-
	Tuesday	Intervals	5 x 1-mile at 10K pace, 90-second jog recovery	8
	Wednesday	Easy Run	40 minutes easy, focus on recovery	4
	Thursday	Off	Swim Focus Day	-
	Friday	Tempo Run	20-minute warmup, 30 minutes at marathon pace, 10-minute cooldown	7
	Saturday	Long Run	90 minutes easy with 6 x 2-minute efforts at 5K pace (2-minute recovery) in the final third	6-7
	Sunday	Off	Bike Focus Day	-
6	Monday	Off	Recovery Swim or Easy Bike	-
	Tuesday	Intervals	4 x 800m at 5K pace, 2-minute jog recovery (reduced volume)	7
	Wednesday	Easy Run	30 minutes recovery pace, focus on staying loose	3
	Thursday	Off	Swim or light bike session to stay active	-
	Friday	Shakeout Run	20 minutes easy with 4 x 30-second strides at marathon pace	4
	Saturday	Off	Rest and focus on hydration and mental preparation	-
	Sunday	Race Day		-

After the first two weeks of building up, it was time for tapering. As many athletes note, this is one of the most psychologically difficult parts of the racing process. With extreme endurance ultradistance events like Ironman, it is necessary to let the body rest and recover in order to replenish depleted stores of glycogen and allow the muscles to build back up to 100 percent. This rest before a big performance is when the body heals in order to produce the results we hope to achieve. At the same time, convincing athletes to rest can be a tough proposition.

It is also often a struggle to keep away from just doing one more workout, one more hard set, just to make sure we are ready to perform. We want to make sure that we can still perform at our desired level on the day. Nerves and anxiety mean that we want to make sure nothing is wrong on the day and that our bodies will be able to handle the stress of racing. We often wrongly figure that the best way to do this is to go out for one more hard workout or even just a moderately hard workout. We think that our bodies will be able to handle it if we go just a bit more, just a bit faster. Unfortunately, all the stress and fatigue that our bodies have accumulated over the previous months (or years) of training can come back to bite us at this most vulnerable moment.

Many endurance athletes preparing for a competition find themselves going out just a bit too hard in the weeks when they are meant to be tapering and end up straining a muscle or tweaking a joint before or on race day. They might have been fine had they sat on the couch eating crisps or gone to get a massage, allowing their bodies to process and rebuild after their hard training.

My body, fortunately, had a quite literally built-in indicator for when I had enough and needed to take a break. The pins in my thigh and hip were especially sensitive when I was fatigued. The more I worked the muscles around them, the more the metal inserts would feel sore and out of place. I could just barely feel the alien body as I ran and cycled, and by the end of the two-week buildup, I knew it was time to sit back and get all the accumulated exhaustion out of my muscles.

We had a meticulously crafted taper designed to peak our fitness for the upcoming race. But as often happens with the best-laid plans, things didn't quite go according to schedule. It all started with Niels. Daily swims were part of the training, but he opted to join a local swim race just before the taper. During the race, Niels was kicked in the eye while drafting behind someone. An unfortunate situation but also not unusual in racing.

After finishing the race, we saw that the injury was serious enough to warrant multiple trips to an emergency optician and raised concerns about potential vision loss.

Meanwhile, Steve and I were feeling the effects of our own intense training schedule. Two weeks of hard work had left us feeling overcooked, our bodies yearning for rest. Between managing Niels' injury and our collective fatigue, we needed to scale back our training massively. I personally cut down my runs to half-hour sessions, maintaining drills but significantly reducing the distance. Cycling and swimming sessions were shortened, and when the guys decided to do a familiarization swim of the race course, I opted to swim only half the distance.

The final week before the race saw a dramatic reduction in training volume. From the thirty hours a week we did during the first two weeks, we dropped down to only twelve two weeks out from the race. Finally, the week before the race, I only did about five hours of training. As I noted at the beginning of this section, the transition from intense training to near inactivity is a mental battle. Though I felt restless and sometimes unsure of how to spend my energy, I knew I had to put those nerves somewhere else. The familiar routine of training sessions was gone. Taking Niels to the hospital only took so many hours each day, so the rest of my time was spent either contacting my coaching clients, catching up with the other members of the NRG coaching team, or zoned out and getting caught up on TV shows I had missed during the heavier blocks of training.

The buildup and taper experience reminded me of the importance of discipline in both training and rest. It taught me the importance of trusting my body and being adaptable. It showed me that even the best-laid plans can be thrown off course and that sometimes the most important step is to take a step back and listen to what your body is telling you. By embracing these insights and adapting to changing conditions, you can navigate the challenges of training and tapering to achieve your full potential on race day.

The power of rest

Leading up to the 1995 Asia Cup, again in Amakusa, I had worked myself into what I thought of as the peak of fitness. My training had been solid, and I was feeling very confident I could take the top of the podium. The week before the race, however, I felt a sudden urge to pull back. I was doing 5 x 1,600m (5 x one-mile). I finished the first two intervals in four minutes, forty-five seconds. I knew I was race-fit, but during the intervals, my back felt very tight—I was still struggling with the injury from two years prior. As I lined up for the third interval, I listened to my body and just stopped and went home. I drastically reduced the rest of my training volume until race day. I basically kicked my feet up for a week, only doing very light jogs and some stretching.

It was a risky move, going against conventional wisdom—at that time, coaches and trainers all thought it was smart money to push yourself right up to the edge. But as I stood on the starting line, I felt a calmness wash over me. I knew I had done everything I could to prepare, and now it was time to trust my body.

The race unfolded beautifully. I ran a personal best for a 10K—just under thirty-one minutes, exceeding my expectations, winning the race, and the best time I've ever run in a triathlon. That experience taught me a valuable lesson: Sometimes the most important training session is the one you don't do. In the end, training makes you weaker. It's in the recovery that we become stronger. Even now, I take special care to get enough rest and relaxation to counteract the potential for injury while letting my body recover enough to achieve peak performance.

Takeaways:

- **Listen to your body:**
  It's crucial to recognize the signs of overtraining and adjust your training accordingly.
- **Embrace adaptability:**
  Plans are meant to be flexible and should be adjusted based on your individual needs and circumstances.
- **Focus on the big picture:**
  While the urge to train may be strong, remember that sometimes the most important training session is the one you don't do.
- **Draw on past experiences:**
  Learn from past successes and failures to make informed decisions about your training and race preparation.

Additional Tips:

- **For first-time athletes:**
  Don't hesitate to seek guidance from experienced athletes and coaches who can help you navigate the challenges of training and tapering.
- **Remember, less is often more:**
  During the final weeks before a race, focus on quality over quantity. Short, focused training sessions can be more beneficial than long, drawn-out ones.
- **Find other ways to fill your time:**

When you step back from training, it's important to find other activities that you enjoy. This will help you stay focused and motivated while also allowing your body to recover.

6

Kona Ironman Race 2022

Pre-race preparation had me fiddling with the nutrition gels, pinning my number, and rehearsing the swim-bike-run mantra in my head. But the real preparation, the kind that calmed the storm within and filled me with quiet confidence, happened in my bed the night before. Years of racing have taught me the value of a pre-race ritual. This wasn't just about checking my kit—though my bike was strategically nestled in transition, third rack, Coca-Cola side, helmet secured. It was about mentally running the course, brick by mental brick.

I lay there, eyes closed, and dived into the cool water, feeling the goggles snug on my face. Out I'd surge, skin slick and ready, then I'd run up the ramp to my bike, helmet, and sunglasses, shoes clicking into pedals as I power down the familiar course. The run was no different. I traced the path in my mind's eye, feeling the tarmac under my shoes, the wind both blowing in my face and at my back. Every mile and kilometre marker, every landmark, was etched into the mental map that would guide me on race day.

The biggest stressor, surprisingly, wasn't the race itself. I knew the importance of hydration, pacing, and proper recovery. My fear was that I would commit a rookie mistake—a lack of contingency for unforeseen issues. I needed to be prepared for every eventuality: spare tire for a puncture, tools for a slipped chain, comfortable socks to prevent blisters, extra gels and salt tabs in my pocket in case I drop one along the way. Every base needed covering, every error eliminated. The leg, with its constant ache, was the only reason I might consider pulling out, and I didn't want to give myself any other possible excuse.

As I woke before dawn on October 8, 2022, I thought back on all I had come through to get there. The leg break, the surgery, the rehabilitation, the move, all of the major changes in half a year's time. All of this preparation had brought me here. The only thing left to do was execute the plan.

Morning arrived, and the usual pre-race frenzy was replaced by a serene calm. No frantic searching for a missing kit, just a cup of coffee and a simple breakfast of white rice and jam—my body's familiar fuel. We'd prepped meticulously, loaded the car, and Rieko had dropped us at the starting line. Then came the chaos of transition: body marking, queueing, water bottles, tire pumps, last-minute checks. The transition area was a frenzy with volunteers barking orders and panicked athletes rushing about. We already knew the route like the back of our hands, so while others pushed and shoved, we mentally rehearsed the race, brick by mental brick. Each swim stroke, pedal turn, and stride was visualized, calming the storm within and building a quiet confidence.

As I stood on the start line in the dark, I knew this ritual wasn't just about preparation. It was about trust. I trusted myself, my training, and the mental rehearsal that had already carried me across the finish line. I was going to finish this race and show everyone and myself that I had truly recovered into something and someone tougher than iron.

The start was a slow affair. Age groups shuffled nervously, no one eager to jump into the cool water. But after the initial plunge, I found myself unexpectedly leading the pack in my starting group. It was a strange sensation, but I knew it wasn't sustainable. My training hadn't been optimal, and pushing too hard now would only spell disaster later. So, I eased back, drafting off the leaders and settling into a comfortable pack not far behind Steve.

Then, disaster struck: a cramp in my leg. Panic threatened to spike my heart rate and flood my body with stress hormones, but I remembered my pre-race mantra: "Don't panic; it won't help." I adjusted my pace, letting the leaders go, choosing a slower but steady pace to prevent a fiery crash. The cramp lingered, a nagging reminder of my limitations, but I held on to the turning point, hoping it would unclench and let me even out my stroke. At the turn, rolling on my back for ten seconds of rest helped my body deliver much-needed oxygen to the cramping limb, and I was able to continue without any more breaks. I found my stroke rhythm again and headed back toward Kailua Bay.

I was sixth out of the water, but the first transition was another hurdle.

My bag was missing, replaced with a stranger's. Precious minutes ticked by while volunteers scurried to rectify the mistake. Frustration burned, but again, I forced myself to reframe the situation. A minute lost is a drop in the Ironman bucket, and panicking wouldn't win back the time.

I found my rhythm on the bike. While riders surged past, I held my ground, aware my training hadn't prepared me to break any records. I had calculated the wattage I could hold for the duration of the race at a modest 170. This would give me an average speed of roughly thirty kilometres per hour, which would see me back to the bike-run transition in six hours. My sessions on the trainer and more recently on the road told me I could hold out that long. I locked onto that number and set my engine to run at the target pace, passing the airport, crossing the familiar lava fields, up to Hawi, and turning around to do it all again. I knew the watts on my bike computer wouldn't lie, and my aero position was dialled to help me cut through the air with minimal resistance. The early wave of competitors overtaking me had me worried, but then the headwind whipping through town on the return leg brought a surprise: I began passing people. It hit me—many of those early flyers must have blown up, and my conservative approach was paying off. I pumped away for five hours and fifty-eight minutes, finally hitting my goal of sub-six hours.

Pedalling away on race day

Let's get one thing straight regarding peeing on your bike during an Ironman: This is officially and strictly not allowed. But here's the thing: To race well, we need adequate hydration, and there's only so much liquid we'll lose through sweat unless we want to dry ourselves out. Holding it all in while you churn away on two wheels is a fast track to discomfort, and when you're already uncomfortable from the extended exercise, that can lead to disaster. So, while I wouldn't exactly recommend breaking any rules mid-race, let's just say I ensured my internal reservoir was adequately drained before tackling the bike leg, and I had ample evidence that I wasn't dehydrated before dismounting at Transition 2. Call it paranoia, call it strategic planning, but I prefer to avoid feeling like a waterlogged sponge by the time I hit the run.

Smiling through the pain

The run started like a nightmare. The legs refused to cooperate, forcing me to walk, jog, walk again. But slowly, miraculously, they came alive. I found my rhythm, a steady 5:30-per-kilometre (8:50/mile) pace, and held it. The heat climbed, pushing my heart rate toward danger, but the ice-cold sponges handed to me by volunteers kept my core temperature in check.

The podium was out of reach, but that didn't matter. My mind was set on cracking eleven hours, more for the personal challenge than anything else. Dismounting the bike, I braced for the usual leg-fire, but a wave of leaden silence greeted me instead. My legs wouldn't budge. Panic threatened to bubble up, but years of racing had taught me a different strategy. I walked. Slowly, deliberately, feeling my body reawaken. A hundred metres, a stretch, a jog, then repeat. The rhythm built, hesitant at first, then steady, until the familiar thrum of my gait returned. I again locked into a 5:30 pace, a tempo that felt comfortable, sustainable. I knew I wanted to keep my heart rate as close to 120 as possible. The heat was on the horizon, and I knew I needed a reserve.

Confidence, however, was my fuel. I had the biggest engine in that race, a resting heart rate of twenty-seven—back down to where it was in university. My resting pulse even now is only thirty beats per minute. This meant I had a massive stroke volume—the ability to push oxygen to my muscles with brutal efficiency. I had tested my max heart rate at around 170, so I knew I had to keep it comfortably below 140. That was the boundary where heat exhaustion lurked, and I knew I needed to watch for that. Checking my watch. With each ice-cold sponge, my core temperature dipped, drawing blood away from my overheated periphery and back to the vital organs.

It was a balancing act, this internal symphony. Aerobic respiration, which provides literal air conditioning for the blood and organs by moving out heated carbon dioxide, was helping me get through. My body was a finely tuned machine after all these months and years, and it knew how to do what I was demanding. After that, it was just the relentless drive to the finish line. I maintained, mile after mile, the mantra of steady effort echoing in my head. I ran not for a podium but for the triumph of will, the quiet satisfaction of keeping the promise to myself. I could bounce back from anything, and I knew I was going to bounce back all the way to the finish line.

My pace, aimed at a sub-four-hour marathon, felt precarious yet sustainable. With 10km remaining, I made a conscious decision: no more risks. Podiums weren't my priority today. I wouldn't gamble with my race, wouldn't flirt with disaster. My focus was maintaining, not exceeding. I slowed down. My carefully calibrated heart rate, hovering between 120 and 140, had served me well for the entire race. Even with 10km to go, I felt I had another gear. Five minutes, maybe ten, could be shaved off. But the allure of pushing harder was tempered by the chilling spectre of "blowing up"—collapsing on the course, the chance to finish slipping through my fingers. I was teetering on the edge, and I knew it.

Fuelling this cautious determination was the meticulous pre-race strategy I'd crafted. Each aid station became a pit stop, a well-oiled routine. Run in, grab the water, ice, and a blissful swig of cola—a heavenly antidote to the bike-induced sports drink fatigue. A Red Bull, however, proved a misstep, its potent caffeine and taurine an unwelcome jolt—my heart rate spiked just after I drank it, and I'll refrain from commenting on the flavour. I switched back to the trusty cola, sports drink, and gels. They were all undeniably effective.

My legs hurt something awful, but by the end, everything else was joining the party. Blistered foot, shoulder tangoing with the handlebars, back screaming from running after holding the aero position—it was a full-body chorus of pain. The rods probably raised the pain volume a notch, but it was still fascinating how the leg, the supposed MVP of pain to that point, just blended into the background. Everything else had its own show to put on at that moment, so I couldn't pay attention to any one thing. Step by painful step, I made my way down Queen Ka`ahumanu Highway toward the crowds at the finish on Ali`i Drive, the sun just starting to dip toward evening. I had been going for well over ten hours, more than nine and a half relying on my legs to push me forward.

I hit the finish line and collapsed, an exhausted mess. As I rolled on my back on the blue carpet, a wave of elation washed over me. I'd done it. From broken-legged hospital patient to Ironman finisher in less than a year. My body, apparently deciding it had had enough of my games, threw in the towel. Cramps erupted, and suddenly, I was on a one-way trip to the medical tent. I must have really been running on fumes. So, lesson learned: Listen to your body, even if it whispers instead of shouts. And maybe, just maybe, pack an extra layer of hydration insurance.

The pit crew swarmed, administering an IV and wrapping me in ice to stave off heatstroke. Turns out, even though I didn't *feel* dehydrated, an IV drip was needed to keep me from drying out completely. Once I came to, the anticlimactic reality hit. I faced the logistical beast of post-race life: retrieving my bike, finding my waiting family, packing up the gear, and driving home for a well-earned collapse into bed. It was a stark contrast to the adrenaline cocktail of the finish, a reminder of the physical and mental war I'd waged against myself and the course.

Post race, post IV drip, feeling successful

In that moment, my mind raced back to the journey, the broken leg, the gruelling rehab, the doubt that gnawed at my spirit, and the sheer, unwavering determination that had carried me through. A lump formed in my throat as I remembered my friend Steve, who'd battled alongside me. I'd caught him on the run, but he'd faced an unseen enemy: COVID.

We'd joked that the only person who could beat me was my best mate, but the reality of his struggle was bittersweet. He finished, walking the marathon with a grit that would put most heroes to shame, but the virus had sapped his strength. I lay there at the finish, waiting for him, the image of his determination having fuelled my own through the race. Perhaps I even drifted off to sleep as I waited, a well-earned respite after pushing my limits to their very edges.

This finish line wasn't just about crossing a physical barrier; it was about conquering the demons within. From the shattered bone to the relentless training, I'd defied expectations and emerged stronger. The joy of accomplishment mingled with the humility of realising the true meaning of the Ironman: not just speed but resilience, grit, and the will to never give up. This wasn't about proving anyone wrong; it was about proving myself right. I learned that slow and steady wins the race and that walking wasn't a failure but a testament to my unyielding spirit. I found my own definition of Ironman: pushing my limits while honouring my body and crossing the finish line with my head held high, knowing I gave it everything I had.

While I couldn't have done it without my professional triathlon background, experience alone wasn't enough. Yes, I knew the course, the demands, and what it took to qualify. But equally crucial was my self-awareness: I knew my body and the mental fortitude required. Saying "anyone can do it" isn't quite accurate. Completing an Ironman requires a whole support system beyond just personal strength.

It's not just about pushing yourself; it's about the meticulous groundwork laid before the event. Years of coaching and racing experience, careful training plans, and the expertise of physios—all these pieces had to be in place. While there are any number of people who have the raw talent and time to do this, the sheer determination that pulled me through is what makes this story unique. I had just turned sixty! Watching friends and former training partners hang up their shoes along the way, I knew that I had to do something special to get me to this point.

That's what makes this journey so unique, but it wouldn't be complete without acknowledging my wife's immense sacrifice. She believed in me, drove me to countless training sessions, and took on countless household burdens. While I was buried in rehab, she was the quiet engine keeping everything running: cooking, cleaning, and offering unwavering support. I've mentioned before how indebted I am to Rieko for everything, but I'll stress it here again.

The move to New Zealand added another layer of complexity. Selling a house, packing a life, and navigating a new healthcare system—these weren't just logistical hurdles; they were potential derailers. It wasn't just about Kona; it was about a new chapter in our lives, a leap into the unknown.

So, yes, while finishing the Ironman was a testament to my physical and mental resilience, it was also a victory for the incredible support system that held me up. Every piece, from years of training to the friends who got me through to my wife's unwavering love, played its part in this extraordinary puzzle. This journey wasn't just about crossing a finish line; it was about proving that even the most ambitious dreams can take flight when supported by the right wind.

Takeaway lessons:

- **The importance of mental preparation:**
  Visualization and mental rehearsal can be powerful tools for managing pre-race anxiety and building confidence.
- **Flexibility and adaptability:**
  Even with meticulous planning, unexpected challenges can arise during a race. Being able to adjust your strategy on the fly is crucial.
- **The power of pacing and self-awareness:**
  Knowing your limits and sticking to a sustainable pace can be the difference between finishing strong and not finishing at all.
- **The role of support systems:**
  Having a strong support network, both on and off the course, can provide invaluable physical and emotional assistance.
- **The significance of post-race recovery:**
  Proper recovery, including hydration, nutrition, and rest, is essential for bouncing back after an Ironman.

7

This is How I Recover?

The day after the race, I could barely walk—Rieko took a video of how I could barely get down the stairs at the rental property. Fans of my Instagram page can scroll back a bit and find it. The next days were a mess of attempting to stretch, getting enough salt, hydration, and minerals back into my body to move it toward equilibrium, and revelling in the delayed onset muscle soreness (DOMS) that had become so familiar to me across my sporting career.

Struggling with the stairs again

After my return to New Zealand, I spent several weeks recovering. It took about a week to get back to the place where I felt my body had processed all the fatigue, but I was reminded of why professional Ironman-distance racers only do a limited number of races per year. I know that I can take a week to ten days off without compromising my fitness level, so I made the most of this time. I still got out and did a light jog or swim most days, but some days I even left my sports watch at home. No point in documenting these runs or swims as they weren't going to be fast and wouldn't measurably affect my fitness level. The point of most of these sessions was simply to keep oxygen flowing to my muscles and remove any remaining trace of lactate that might have failed to get flushed away. Staying active was going to be key because I knew the story had to continue.

The whispers of the 2023 Championships had started swirling in my head. Controversially, the race in 2023 would be held in Nice, France rather than in its traditional home in Kona. This decision by the organizing committee is still receiving a great deal of criticism at the time of this writing, and I won't throw out an opinion on the politics of everything here. I will make a personal statement that while I had enjoyed my time in Hawaii before the race, I was just as happy to visit a new location. Part of the joy of racing for me is getting to see new courses and getting to know new locations. Perhaps this comes from my earlier days of adventuring. In any case, I was excited about the prospect of going to Europe to train and compete.

After the Championships in the autumn of 2022, I saw I could build myself up strong enough to finish the Ironman in less than six months. *What could I do with a proper year to prepare?* I wondered. From broken to champion had a nice ring to it, and I was going to find out what grit and determination could do. Could I get on the podium? Take the top spot? Or maybe dare to dream—build myself up to claiming a world record?

It was during this period that I decided to join my wife at her CrossFit training playground. I had always joined gyms on my own or occasionally dragged friends out for strength sessions. However, CrossFit had me from day one. I could forget those lonely gym sessions of the past and enjoy camaraderie and healthy competition every time I visited. I was surrounded by folks pushing their limits, and it was infectious. I packed on almost five kilograms of muscle, melted away my body fat down to eleven percent, and felt stronger than ever. As a very social person, for me, it has always been about more than just the workouts. The whole community of people supporting each other and having fun along the way really drove me to get strong.

The next step would be to use these newfound muscles for more than in-house competitions and winning weekly parkruns. Normally, I could have picked any race in the world and had a good chance of snatching a top-ten age-group spot, but time wasn't my ally. I was preparing to have the rods in my thigh removed in April, then it was a six-week sprint of rehab and strength training, a desperate scramble to rebuild my shattered body. If all went well, it would be pins out, crutches on, and back to rehab, then on to the World Championships.

I had a limited number of shots to qualify for the Championships in Nice before April. Ironman New Zealand, my main gatekeeper, awaited me in March. There wouldn't be much room for another qualifying race—I would have to hold onto the fitness and strength I had gained for Kona and build speed and strength to get a top slot. Qualifying wouldn't be a given. My mate Steve Farrell would be in the mix too and racing in the same age group, as well as numerous other very competent contenders. I would need to pull out a much stronger performance than in October 2022 in order to compete well on the world stage again.

Fortunately, upon my return, we were entering the summer season in Auckland, which meant ideal temperatures and conditions for training. Even better, there would be a number of local races that would still take my registration over the next few months. I put my name down for all of them, from the weekly parkruns to the National Championships.

Ironman racing has never been my main calling. I had set out two years before to race at the top of my age group, ideally finishing in the top 5 competitors. After that, the plan was to go back to the shorter distances where I truly thrived. Fortunately, I could do that while still keeping my Ironman goals in sight. By registering for every big and small race I could around New Zealand, I could set a reasonable schedule for myself and have fairly reliable measures of my performance at the longer and shorter distances.

In February, Steve, some other friends, and my family and I planned a trip down to Taupo for a weekend of racing. We had registered for the National Aquathlon Championships, a local sprint race, and a reconnaissance ride of the Ironman course to prepare for April—each a steppingstone toward the IM Worlds in Nice. The plan was meticulously

orchestrated, from races to the locations where we stayed. No more sudden changes from our rental hosts either—this time it seems karma caught up to us and we got a lucky break instead.

Rieko was brilliant in securing the best accommodations for all of our trips. Upon arrival in Taupo, however, we were uncertain of the house. Was it this one or the one up the road? Both had the same number on the box but different digits after the hyphen. Undeterred, we walked up to the door, located the lockbox, and punched in the code we had been given. With a click and a clunk, it worked! We thought we had the key. The front door opened to leather couches, gleaming flatscreen televisions, and shelves groaning under the weight of vintage novels—this was no ordinary rental. This was a sanctuary of exquisite taste, a testament to its owner's impeccable standards. We tiptoed through the unfamiliar splendour, marvelling at the whiskey decanter glinting in the afternoon light and

wondering if we'd stumbled into a scene from a particularly luxurious reality show.

The next day at the aquathlon race venue, a seed of doubt sprouted in my wife's mind. A double-check of the address confirmed her worst fears: It turned out those numbers after the hyphen had been rather crucial. The realisation dawned on us that we were camped out in the wrong house. After we finished the race (with another age group top-spot finish for me), we hurried back to the rental and made sure to clean everything meticulously. We were pretty certain that the house we stayed in was the owners' private getaway.

Nerves gnawed at our insides as we returned and cleaned up. As we were finishing the laundry, we heard a car pull up outside. Fortunately, instead of the fiery wrath of a homeowner wronged, we were met with laughter and genuine amusement. The owners were a charming couple with a penchant for adventure and, apparently, identical lockbox codes on all of their properties. They regaled us with tales of past Airbnb mishaps—it sounded like ours wasn't the worst they'd suffered. They marvelled at our meticulous housekeeping, particularly my valiant attempt to mend their broken vacuum cleaner with nothing but sheer determination. They led us to the *correct* house for our stay and wished us the best with the remaining races that weekend.

Sometimes you can't go back home

Cleaning house at the Airbnb reminded me of another time a house party got a bit out of control.

After my adventures in the United States in 1985, I mentioned that I had hit a low point, but that wasn't the whole story. I returned to the UK and decided to throw a party at my parents' house while they were out of town. However, things quickly spiraled out of control and the party got out of hand. My friend, who had been given the keys to the house, let in a group of people and before we knew it, the house was trashed, with food stolen from the fridge and Christmas ornaments smashed.

As if that wasn't bad enough, I was drunk when I returned home and tripped on the doorstep, slicing my ear on the glass front door. A friend rushed me to the hospital, where my ear was stitched back together and reattached. However, I didn't realize that my parents were actually in England and had returned home to find the house in disarray and their son missing. When they tracked me down at the hospital, my dad told me to sort myself out. Until I did, I wouldn't be welcome at home. It was a low point for me, and I knew that I needed to make some changes in my life.

As I struggled to get my life back on track, I was staying on my older sister's sofa. After a few days there, she suggested that I apply to become a physical education teacher. Her boyfriend at the time encouraged me to do so as well. He told me that when I had my interview, I should just say that teaching was all I had ever wanted to do and I would be accepted.

Feeling desperate and with little else to lose, I took his advice and applied for the teaching license programme at Leeds

University. To my surprise, I was accepted and spent a year training to become a PE teacher.

During this darker period following my return to England with my knee injury, I had put on some extra weight. I knew that an overweight PE instructor was a nonstarter, so I began to focus on nutrition and diet for the first time. Now in my twenties, I could no longer eat and drink as I liked. It was during this time that I really learned the ins and outs of nutrition, especially how it would work for me. I studied my lessons as seriously as I could and worked on getting fit. It was another turning point for me. I was finally able to make some positive changes and began building a healthy base for my next set of adventures in Japan and beyond.

Back to the story of the race, I pushed myself hard in the Aquathlon National Championships. The 1,000m swim left me feeling stiff, but I unleashed a very strong run, clocking the third-fastest run-course time of the day. Unfortunately, the early swim deficit proved too great. Had I shaved off just a few seconds by swimming a bit straighter, pulling a bit harder, I could have snagged third overall. Still, I was finishing fifth overall at sixty just a year after my injury and with a leg still cobbled together with bits of metal. The third-fastest run felt like no small feat on that hilly course.

Unfortunately, the next day during the sprint-distance triathlon race, disaster struck. My swim came off without a hitch as I clocked a similar time to the previous day but still felt good. During the bike leg, as we were coming around a hairpin, a younger rider overtook me and carelessly clipped my front tire. The moment my tire wobbled, I knew I was going down. Adrenaline slowed my perspective, and I had a moment to think *Not again! At least not on the right side!* I swerved the opposite way and went down on the opposite side. My left wrist hit first and took the brunt of the impact before I rolled onto my left hip, leaving me with road rash and a broken hand. I stood up, feeling the familiar numbness and radiating wrongness of another break. All of the bones along the outside of my forearm and hand were lit up with that throbbing ache I remembered so well from the year before.

I stood in the road clutching my wrist and watching the racers streaming by as I tried to manoeuvre out of their way. The young man who had hit my tire was long out of sight, as were my chances of finishing this race. *Sixty years of life and I did everything but break a bone, now twice in less than a year,* I thought. Disappointed, I picked up my bike and moved off the road.

As I got out of the way of the racers, I noticed a girl looking roughly the same age as my daughter coming up the road. "I saw you fall. Do you need help?" she asked.

"Yes, my hand's broken," I said. She quickly punched a number in her phone.

"You know it's broken?" she asked.

"Yes, I'm sure," I said. I remembered the exact feeling of wrongness from the break in my leg and had the same sort of feeling coming off my wrist. The girl relayed the information to the race officials and got an ambulance to come to the location. I made a mental note to thank her parents for being so conscientious in raising their daughter and to make sure my own daughter would be able to do the same in a similar situation.

Initially, an ambulance brought me to the hospital and ran all the familiar tests. Rieko and Steve played the key roles of organizing pickups for my bike and other racing equipment and then checked us out of the rental. We were unfortunately quite a ways from a major hospital, so I was taken to a local trauma unit to get patched up. On top of all of this, just after the race finished all the other racers also needed to book it out of town as well: All of New Zealand was now on high alert from a major tropical storm.

The doctors at this small local hospital did the best they could. X-rays confirmed the fracture; I had five fractures in my radius, just below the hand. The bones shifted, so they needed to be realigned and pinned. Luckily, the wrist joint wasn't damaged, and the doctors opted for a permanent titanium plate instead of a temporary carbon one. So, even after the pins come out, I'd still have a little 'Titanium Man' souvenir!

The emergency specialist on call was adamant that I would need another set of pins in the hand to properly stabilize the healing. The plan was to transfer me to a larger rural hospital for surgery. With a cyclone warning hitting New Zealand at this time, this would mean another week in Taupo until a surgeon could be reached. I told the hospital staff that my surgeon at Auckland's North Shore Hospital was already prepped and ready if I could get back. With medically trained friends in the right places willing to vouch for me and the willingness to drive back to Auckland, I got the okay to head back north with a temporary cast and a CT scan awaiting me.

The cyclone warning made progress on the roads quite slow. We took turns driving, enduring the five-hour journey through the storm. After several gruelling and painful hours on the road, I finally made it to the North Shore in Auckland.

Along the way, I started to get the feeling that I might be able to cope with just a decent cast and some extra ibuprofen. I had just broken it and was feeling okay to take my turn driving, so was thinking I might even be able to avoid surgery and the requisite rehab. It was just as this endorphin-fuelled thought was passing through my mind that a friend who broke his radius thirty years ago called, and he offered some valuable advice. He suffers from chronic arthritis now, especially when swimming, and he urged me to get the plate. He said the pain could be debilitating, and at our age, we needed to prioritise long-term body health. After all, winning the 95-100 age group wouldn't be much fun with arthritis! That completely changed my mind. I took the long view and decided to ensure my body would be well-equipped for years to come. The plate was going to be the best option.

American Adventures Part 1: Delivering the rustbucket

The drive up the coast reminded me of another fraught journey. Back in 1984, I was twenty-one, fresh from winning the university 1,500m national title, with a gold medal in hand and a bit of a chip on my shoulder. I have mentioned earlier that my dream was to see the Los Angeles Olympics in person, but funds were tight. I'd scraped together enough for a single ticket to New York on Laker Airways, the Freddie Laker, but had no plan for how to get across the country. I was young and full of optimism, treating the 5,000-kilometre journey as a grand adventure

On the flight to New York, I quickly realised I'd need to make connections if I was going to get to LA. By sheer luck, I met two college lecturers who were taking 'drive-away' cars across the country—essentially a free way to transport vehicles for wealthy owners. They invited me to join them, and I jumped at the chance. Our first car was a 1970s Pontiac Firebird, a real rust bucket. It seemed odd that someone would want such a clunker transported to Louisiana, but I wasn't complaining. The plan was to pick up another car in New Orleans and head west from there

The journey took an unexpected turn when we had a flat tyre on a remote stretch of road. As we changed the tyre, we discovered several bricks of white powder hidden in the car's compartments. It didn't take a genius to figure out what we'd stumbled upon. My friends wanted to go to the police, but I was terrified. What if the people behind this operation were watching us? The safest option seemed to be delivering the car as planned, so we agreed to act as if nothing had happened

The drive through Louisiana's swamplands was tense. Every mile felt heavier with the weight of what we were unknowingly involved in. Once in New Orleans, we discreetly handed over the car and left without a word. Looking back, I'm still torn. Did we prioritise survival over doing the right thing? Absolutely. But the fear of crossing dangerous people outweighed any moral obligation at that moment. It's a life lesson I carry with me—a reminder that some decisions are made not in black and white but in the murky grey of survival.

Back in Auckland, the surgeon confirmed the need for surgery, but the hospital was fully booked for the weekend. We had arrived on a Saturday, so my operation was rescheduled for the following Monday. The surgeon, aware of my daily exercise routine, assured me that the titanium plate and lightweight cast would allow me to get back on track after just two weeks. Swimming would be out of the question, but at least I wouldn't be chained to crutches like before. I could still run or turn my legs on the indoor cycle as long as I didn't push too hard.

From national championship aspirations to a broken arm, my journey had taken an unexpected turn. I decided this would be just another chapter in the story of how I eventually rebounded stronger than before. With the titanium rods in my leg and the plate now in my hand, I truly could own the title of Titanium Man. Now I just needed to really conquer the Ironman.

Training around my broken wrist

After my surgery on my arm in late February, I turned to the question of races. Knowing that the Ironman race in April in Taupo was out of the question, my focus shifted to Ironman Cairns in June. I contacted the organizers, begging them to let me switch my New Zealand entry, but rules were rules so it seemed. After a week of back and forth on the phone, asking to speak with different race organizers, I finally got a definitive 'no.' Prior experience even in Japan told me that there are times and places where the regulations were hard and fast, and other times and places where things were more flexible if you dealt with the right person. While I had hoped for the latter, it turned out to be the former.

With a month to go until the rods came out in March, I buckled down to get as much time in on the indoor trainer as possible. I needed to pump my aerobic fitness levels as high as I could get them, and that meant more than six hours on the indoor bike trainer on some days. I maintained my stretching and drills as best as I was able and used all of the stairs I could find in Auckland (not a stretch!) to do low-impact running. The road to the World Championships might be on a detour, but my wheels were still spinning, and I wasn't going to stop until I crossed that finish line.

My social media family was very divided. Some were cheering me on as if I was on the verge of conquering Everest, while others were whispering doubts about my creaky, sixty-year-old bones and slowing pace. Let me tell you, I'm firmly in the 'never say never' camp. Recalculate, adjust, push through—that's my mantra.

It was just before my surgery that I received a piece of well-timed news. My entry from 2020 for the cancelled Ironman race in Taiwan had granted me a transfer to any race in Asia. While I couldn't get them to transfer it to Cairns, I got a shot at a race in Subic Bay in the Philippines in June. This would line up nicely with some work I had lined up with a new shoe company in Indonesia called Ortuseight. I began preparing my rehabilitation and recovery schedule to match not only the Ironman in the Philippines but also with an eye on the race in Nice.

I was confident I could qualify for the Championships given past performances but also due to the unpopularity of the race locale. Many who might have traditionally gone to Kona for the Hawaiian vacation were foregoing their qualification spots, so slots in many age groups were going unfilled. Many triathletes outside Europe didn't necessarily know Nice and southern France as an equivalent area of warm beaches and beautiful scenery, but I had no qualms about profiting from their loss. My hope was that both Steve Farrell and I could get a qualifying spot at this race once I fully recovered.

The pins in my thigh were removed at the end of March 2023. Going in for the procedure was much less painful this time around. For one thing, my body was whole and in one piece! Getting prepped again for surgery less than a month after they had put the plates in my wrist, I felt like I was becoming an old hand at the surgery game. With my left wrist wrapped up in the cast, I went in to the North Shore hospital again in Auckland.

Afterward, the surgeons noted the care and ability with which the Japanese surgeons had inserted the rod in my thigh. It seems I was fortunate to have a well-trained surgeon on Ishigaki Island. Both the method and the materials used were high quality, I was told. It gave me a good feeling to know that I had been well-treated and taken care of. Perhaps it even contributed to how I was able to recover so quickly and get back my strength and mobility. In any case, with the pins out of my leg, I was now back in recovery mode.

The first week was spent on crutches as usual. The surgeons were able to remove the rather large and surprisingly heavy piece of metal from my thigh (see photo below). There is naturally damage and pain during any surgery, and I did everything I could to keep from popping my stitches. No swimming, cycling, or running for the first ten days as a guard against infections, but I was now well-versed in finding ways to stay fit, even while only using one leg and one arm.

The rods and screws that were holding me together weighed roughly 240 grams, which is about the same as the rear derailleur or gear cassette on a mid to high-end bicycle. Cyclists have a reputation for being 'weight weenies,' seeking to make the lightest bike they can to help them turn every ounce of strength into forward movement. Adding 240 grams to their bike would be beyond the pale. For runners, 240 grams is about the weight of one racing (running) shoe. I sometimes wondered if I should train with the rod strapped onto my downtube as a reminder that I was carrying it around inside me for a year, and it was weight I couldn't ever take off.

After the months in hospital the previous year and the muscles I had built from CrossFit now coming through, I knew how to maintain my fitness. I could fortunately still use the left leg and right arm, and that was how I kept myself somewhat sane. As I mentioned, tapering and recovering are very hard for athletes. We always want to do a bit more, go a bit harder, but resting and allowing our bodies to use the energy for building muscle

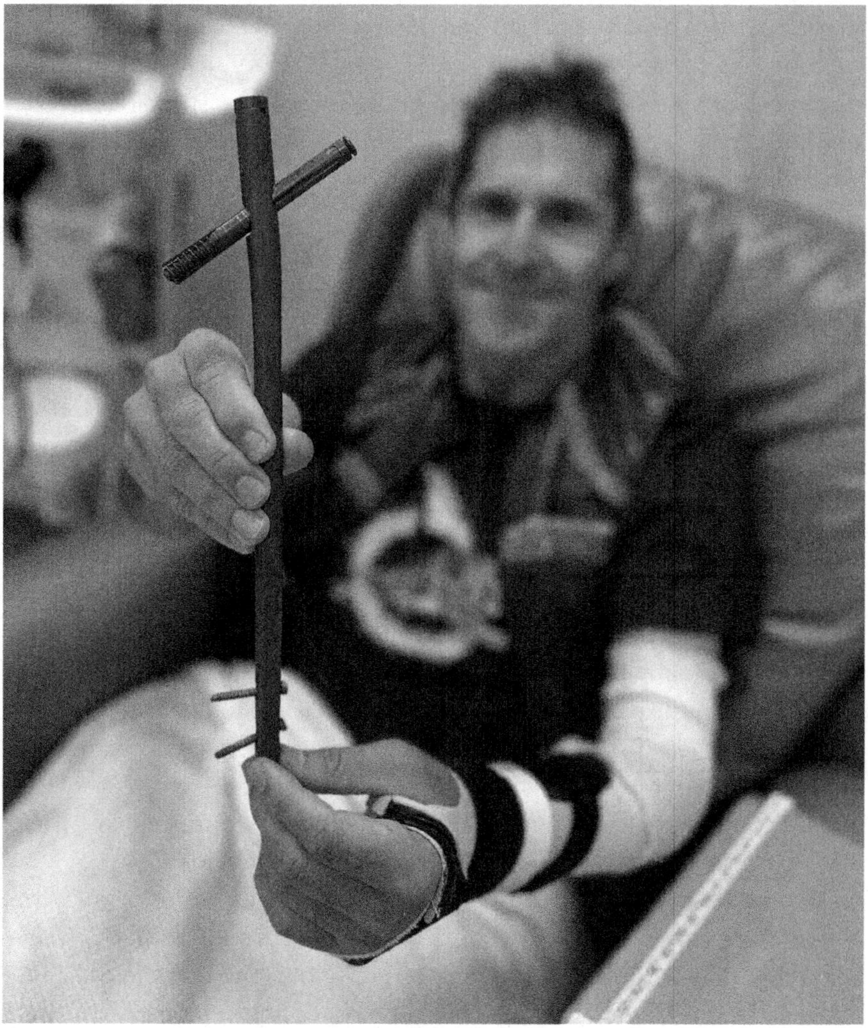

The pins that held my femur together

and bone feels strange. I have fortunately always had a fairly easy time getting to bed at night and getting up early, so sleeping wasn't a problem, but the other sixteen hours a day could sometimes be a struggle.

Just as when I tapered for Kona, and when I was stuck in bed in the hospital on Ishigaki, I threw myself into coaching and the online world. I responded to my posts on Instagram, talked my athletes through their training plans and progress, and kept up with my chess games. Spending time with our daughter and our dog was also a way to keep me feeling good about things. Those positive endorphins from the things that make me happy were a major part of what got me through the previous recovery periods and helped me here as well. Just as before, the hardest thing about being on Instagram is seeing all my athletes post their successes and struggles at races and workouts. I had to keep reminding myself that I would be back to enjoying the full freedom of my body soon, too, but I still needed to complete a thorough recovery.

I did my last parkrun with my pins on March 25, coming in with a decent time of 18:37. I was able to return to this race three weeks later on April 15, coming in at 21:05. The loss of nearly three minutes on the course showed me just how hard I was going to have to work. Two weeks later, I pulled myself back to a time of 19:19. While my times now didn't look as impressive as some of my time trials when I was younger, in looking back on both my age and my recovery, I felt no shame in sharing results like this—indeed, no one should ever feel shame in their athletic achievements, no matter how minor. I was building back up, and I knew I still had some faster races left in me.

Now, to get myself ready for the Ironman in the Philippines and then for the ultimate race in Nice, I spent the next month going back and forth between my three disciplines and strength training. I maintain that I could not have recovered so quickly without a good base of muscular fitness. By the beginning of May 2023, my stitches were out and I was now healed to the point that I could swim in the ocean, run a half-marathon, and pedal stroke for stroke on the bike with my friends on all-day rides.

Beginning in May, I had planned to head to Indonesia to work with a new shoe company. My responsibilities there would be to film some commercial materials and record instructional videos on the drills that I use so frequently to maintain my running condition. Ortuseight was offering some great new running shoes, and I was happy to be a part of their team. More importantly, going to Indonesia would allow me to adjust to the heat and prepare for my race in the Philippines. Steve Farrell and I would go to Jakarta and Belitung to work on promotions for the company and then fly to Manila for the Subic Bay race.

Not having any other races lined up between May and the Ironman Championships, I knew this was cutting it quite close. But I was starting to feel solid after the surgeries and setbacks of the previous months. I knew overcoming those things would be the next step on the journey, and it felt like everything was lined up. The only problem: I was starting to get a bit feverish when I got off the plane in Indonesia...

Takeaways:

- **Prioritise rest and active recovery after an Ironman:** Allow your body adequate time to recover and replenish depleted energy stores. Engage in light exercise, such as jogging or swimming, to promote blood flow and aid in the removal of lactic acid.
- **Leverage your existing fitness base to rebuild for future races:** After a period of rest, use your existing aerobic base to gradually increase training intensity and volume as you prepare for your next goal.
- **Strength training is prehab:** Getting stronger will make you more resilient against injuries and illnesses that might otherwise slow you down or stop you altogether.
- **Find ways to stay active, even with limitations:** If you're recovering from an injury or illness, find alternative forms of exercise that allow you to maintain your fitness level without aggravating your condition.
- **Accept Murphy's law when it comes to setbacks:** It's never a good time to have an accident, but many times they seem to happen at the worst possible. Accept the possibility that life will throw obstacles in your path, and set about to get past them toward your dreams.

8

Ironman Philippines Subic Bay:

The Last Chance?

This next chapter offers the run-up to the Subic Bay race and the struggles I went through before I even got to the Philippines. Rather than tell this story as a recollection like the previous chapters, I've chosen to tell it as it unfolded. I've changed things around to the present tense to show just how uncertain everything was. It was something of a ride, shared with my friends, training partners, and co-author the whole way.

30 MAY, 2023

My luck with tropical islands recently seems to be pretty bad.

I'm here in Belitung island working with the shoe maker Ortuseight, doing photo shoots to promote their brand. Steve Farrell, my good friend over the past thirty years of racing, is here with me from Auckland, and we're working on getting our heat adaptation up for the race on June 11. They flew us up to Jakarta for a few days, and now they've brought us here so we can film and do a bit of training and coaching. Steve and I have done three big rides around the island. I wanted to get a bit more work in to secure a spot for the race, but that was looking a bit unlikely at the moment.

It started out in Jakarta when Steve and I decided we were going to do a pretty standard 15km run. I started off fine, feeling warm, but suddenly my heart rate started to spike and I could barely shuffle back to the hotel. I got back and it was all I could do to get my heart back to beating normally while sitting in a cold shower. When it finally came down, Steve and the guys from Ortuseight took me to the hospital.

I've now been to hospital twice in Indonesia. The first one after that run was a bit of a shocker; they didn't even take my temperature when I told them I was feeling hot! They asked me a few questions, and when I told them I had asthma that flares up from time to time, they put me on a saline drip and prescribed an inhaler before sending me on my way. I hoped that some rehydration would help get my core temperature back down, and it seemed to for a bit.

Filming with Ortuseight on Belitung

We came to Belitung a few days ago, and I'll just reiterate what a lovely island this is. The roads here are beautiful for riding—maybe some of the best I've ever been on. The island hosted a G20 summit, and the infrastructure that came from that is really excellent: smooth, new tarmac all the way around the island, and very little traffic. Like much of Southeast Asia, everyone here seems to ride scooters, and there's little fear of crazy drivers running you off the road (or attacking with cleavers). Steve and I have gone out for three long rides, and they've been some of the smoothest I can remember since my leg break. It's been humid and in the low thirties Celsius (high eighties to low nineties Fahrenheit) most days, and coming from the cool of Auckland, it's taken a bit of work to adjust.

Anyway, after the ride yesterday, I was back to the same place that brought me to a hospital in Jakarta; a high heart rate, feverish, and just generally feeling off. I was starting to get worried I had COVID, so Steve and I went to the hospital here on Belitung. Second time lucky, I guess, but the care felt quite a bit better. They spoke great English, took my temperature, checked my blood, tested everything properly. Overall, it's been a good experience; everyone has been quite kind, though I'm still feeling awful. It fortunately isn't COVID, but I might have picked up some sort of flu on the way over, and the heat has just been weakening my body. Now I've got a fever of about thirty-eight degrees (104 Fahrenheit), and I'm just barely holding on. I keep coughing, and it's that nasty, phlegmy wet cough. I can get enough air once I take a hit of the inhaler, but I keep feeling like I need another puff every ten minutes.

COVID isn't gone by any stretch of the imagination, but they ruled that out, so it looks like it's something else. I just don't seem to be able to cool myself down after these rides and runs. I think it's just that my body doesn't know any good ways to cool down in this kind of weather and without cold drinks. All this heat and humidity mean that I'm just reacting badly.

The resort where we're staying is lovely, but it would be a bit easier if there were cold drink machines everywhere like in Japan. They don't seem to have ice anywhere! You'd think with a tropical climate people would want cold drinks, but that doesn't seem to be what they do here. There's plenty of fruit juice, fresh pineapple or coconut, but it always seems to be served at air temperature—and that's bloody hot! It's almost like drinking a hot fruit tea, and when I'm in the middle of a bike ride or run, that's the last thing I want. A fresh coconut is nice for hydration and some electrolytes, but it's nothing like an ice-cold sports drink or cola when you're out and the heat is coming off the tarmac in waves.

The fortunate thing for me right now is that the work of building up fitness for the Ironman is done. I've got almost two weeks to get over this bug, and I'm pretty confident I'll be able to finish. After the rods came out in March, I was worried about being able to rebuild in time. Recovering in time for this race was right at the edge of possibility, but I think the work has been done now and I know I'll finish the race. I don't think I could have prepared any more than I have, and now I guess this is just nature or God or the universe or whatever telling me how I need to taper.

The hard part has been adjusting my cycling and swimming to the pins that are in my wrist now—those aren't coming out for quite a while, if ever. I'm lucky it's not an event like the Tour de France where I'd be leaning on the handlebars, putting stress on my wrists for hours at a time. I actually feel more comfortable down in the aero position, distributing the weight on my elbows rather than leaning on my wrists. My swim is still okay, but having the pins there too has messed with my stroke a bit. I just can't seem to grab as much water as when I had full mobility. I'll still aim to be with the front pack of my AG, but probably not like I was before. It's a bit of a letdown, really, but maybe this is my post-titanium reality. The run won't bother my hand, but the leg is still recovering a bit, and there's some stiffness and soreness.

Right now, the Championships in Nice isn't looking like a popular destination. This means that so long as I finish in a reasonable time for me, I can possibly get a slot in the roll-down if other people don't want to go—Ironman championship rules allow the next qualified competitor to go if one of the top finishers has already qualified or does not want to go. As I said, the work is done, and whatever happens will happen. Who knows, maybe five really strong over-sixty former pros from wherever are planning to use this race as their unannounced comeback—in racing, nothing is ever a given. If that happens, there's nothing to be done. I can only race my best, and to do that, I'll need to be recovered.

This means that for now, I'll just take it easy, rest up today, travel back to Jakarta tomorrow, and then spend a few days taking it easy there while coaching and finishing the promotional shoots. It's always hard for me to take it easy when I'm coaching because I really like to be out there, but I'll trust Steve to keep me honest. Even a coach needs a coach at times, and Steve is as invested in my journey as I am at this point. We'll just have to keep each other on track until race day.

01 JUNE, 2023

A quick sidebar away from Mike telling his own story.

Back in Jakarta, Steve posts a video online sharing the progress of the illness. Steve walks into the hotel room to wake Mike up, and found him still in bed.

Steve: Mike, it's time to hit the pool. Mike?
Mike (face down on his bed): &#$% off, mate.
Steve: I guess that's that then.

Mike is usually the one coming around at five in the morning to wake people up and get out for early morning rides or swims. This shows just how seriously he's been beaten down by whatever is happening in his system. The illness he was complaining about yesterday is clearly getting the better of him. Back to Mike from here on.

02 JUNE, 2023

I'm in hospital now. The doctors finally gave me a diagnosis of mycoplasmic pneumonia. They say this explains everything from the fevers to the coughing I've been suffering for the past few weeks. I must have picked it up during travel.

It's times like this that you question what you are doing and why you are doing it.

It was a kind of a relief to get a diagnosis because I kept thinking, *Am I just going soft?* Lying in this hospital bed in Jakarta, feeling like crap has made me reaffirm to myself that health must come first, even above my desire to succeed at Ironman. The fighter in me still won't give up.

I feel like a sporting version of Dr. Jekyll and Mr. Hyde.

It would be simpler to take the easier option and quit now. The Hyde side of me growls, *You set this challenge to see what is possible, not what is impossible. I don't care if you are sick. Get back on the bike and ride. You're done when I say you're done.* But Dr. Jekyll is telling me, *Rest up. Recover. Take it easy. You have achieved enough in the sporting world over the years. You don't need to take any more risks. Enjoy a slower pace of life.*

Of course, while I must not attempt anything dangerous or reckless, I owe it to myself to keep finding a way to race until there is no more time left. I guess we all wrestle with our Jekylls and Hydes, our voice of reason and voice of ambition.

As the saying goes, "It's not over till the fat lady sings." That way of thinking has allowed me to achieve so much, so I must keep going and searching for a way to get to Nice. I'll search until there are no more options. That is in my DNA.

A broken arm took me off the start line in IM NZ. Now pneumonia has removed me from IM Philippines. I never for one minute expected pneumonia to complicate the plan. I assumed it would be something with the leg or wrist.

This episode also shows that to reach the top, we sometimes need a bit of luck. Surely I am due for a change in luck soon. Maybe I can't get a podium in Nice in September. Maybe I cannot even make it to the start line.

It is now June. I am lying in a hospital bed with a forty-degree Celsius (104 Fahrenheit) fever and pneumonia. They've got me on a drip, and who knows how long it will take to recover.

I have twelve weeks to get over this, get strong again, train, find a qualifying race to compete in, and then qualify. Time is running out, but I am an eternal optimist. Time has not run out yet. I will find a way.

04 JUNE, 2023

Last night, I was released from hospital, went back to my hotel, and just slept. I've been in bed the past two days and unfortunately had to cancel yesterday's coaching and training sessions that I was planning to do with Ortuseight. I promised them I would do another set of sessions sometime in the future. Steve came into my room this morning and said, "You look a mess, but not as much of a mess as you did yesterday." Rather than cancel the scheduled coaching sessions today, I decided to make a go of it. Steve, who had coached the New Zealand Olympic triathlon team, was able to address most of the physical aspects. He had worked personally with the nearly 200 athletes who showed up and demonstrated the physical skills and drills that would improve their running. I wore a mask and spoke to the crowd, but I kept my distance and tried to maintain my energy.

At the end of the session, the support staff from Ortuseight seemed optimistic. "You'll definitely be ready to race next week," one of them told me.

One of the successful shots from that coaching session with Ortuseight

Steve, on the other hand, was a bit less enthusiastic. He said, "While I want you at that starting line more than anything next week, let's not get hopes up. I've been with you since the start of this and I'll stick by you, but we both know that sometimes the best thing you can do for yourself long-term is cut your losses." I took that to heart. While I'm taking it easy, I do admit that the antibiotics are working. I'm coughing a bunch and still struggling to breathe at times, but even just speaking today took a lot out of me. It's about seven p.m. now, so I'm going to bed, hoping that an early sleep will help me get over this properly.

American Adventures 2: The medal that got me out of jail

The heat and fever I endured on that island brought back memories of another sweltering, uncomfortable night. After surviving the perils of transporting a Pontiac "rust bucket" loaded with unexpected cargo to New Orleans, my friends and I felt a rush of relief and decided to celebrate. I'd saved a bottle of duty-free rum for a special occasion, and this seemed like the perfect moment. Mixing it with cola, I thought it would be a harmless way to unwind. But as the night wore on in the French Quarter, the alcohol flowed freely, and we became separated amidst the chaos of the city.

Eventually, I found myself alone on the street, stopped by the police for drunk and disorderly conduct. Before I knew it, I was sitting in a New Orleans jail cell alongside other drunks and vagrants, the full weight of my intoxication bearing down on me. My friends, after sobering up, came to my rescue the next morning. Thinking quickly, they explained to the authorities that I was a British runner recently named to the Olympic team, even showing my collegiate championship medal as proof. It was a peculiar twist of fate that my athletic achievements became my saving grace, convincing the police to release me with a warning.

That night was a harsh lesson, though I was slow to truly learn from it. Over time, I realised the toll such antics took on my body and mind. These days, I stick to a beer or shandy, knowing my limits and avoiding the reckless behaviour of my youth. Reflecting on those experiences, I'm amazed I managed to maintain my athletic career, but I'm grateful for the perspective they gave me. A lesson learned late is still a lesson learned.

06 JUNE, 2023

Steve and I have made it to the Philippines. We are checked into the Airbnb before the race. I'm still coughing, but the antibiotics I've been taking appear to be working. I talked with Steve about the idea of returning to New Zealand rather than continuing on to Manila, but we ultimately decided that this was an "in for the penny, in for the pound" situation. I want to be there to support Steve's final days of training and cheer on my friend, watch him cross the finish line, and see him qualify for the World Championship. In my condition, trying to race is probably beyond me, but the least I can do is be there for someone who has stuck with me through all these years and miles.

10 JUNE, 2023

A few days after arriving in the Philippines, my health has markedly improved. I woke up the previous day feeling a bit better, my temperature down and my cough manageable. I think I'm on the path to recovery. The infection in my lungs has receded. It was definitely touch and go, but a week of forced bed rest brought me back from the edge.

Steve and I met up with Ayaka Faith Suzuki, one of the premier race organizers and triathletes in the Tokyo area. She has travelled to Subic Bay to compete, and she too is aiming for a win. We joined her for a slow 24km ride, following her around the streets of the course to practise a bit but generally taking it slow. The next day, we hit the sea and splashed about for a kilometre. I've been coughing quite a lot the whole time, and I think I worried Faith a bit. She seemed quite concerned about being near me when we got coffee.

Last night, I found my next option to qualify: an Ironman race in Spain. I checked the timeline and it almost seems possible: fly back to New Zealand for a few weeks, rest and recover, train, and then fly off to Spain to get the qualification slot (assuming there aren't too many fast racers from Europe). The big issue here is the timing, jet lag, and physical recovery, and then being able to fly across the world back to France to prepare for the race. Back and forth to Europe twice in almost as many months would be hell on my body. Would I be able to recover again and qualify? And then do it again and race well? This seems unlikely. No, I'll take my shot here in Subic Bay.

This is a calculated risk. As long as my temperature is gone tomorrow morning, I think I will go for an 'honour finish;' I'll simply aim to complete the course with no specific time or position in mind. If I'm really lucky, enough of the Asian competitors will cede their qualification slot, and then the spot will roll down to me.

I racked my bike, prepared the transition area, and laid out my racewear and nutrition for the morning. I had a pasta dinner with Steve and Faith, where we talked and reminisced about the difficulties and issues with racing in Japan. Faith had just left her position as a coordinator for international races at Samurai Sports to focus on coaching and promoting the Women for Tri brand worldwide. Having raced for years around Japan and the rest of the world, she recognizes the difficulties both of organizing races and promoting gender equality in Japan. The race tomorrow will be her first full Ironman-distance race. She has been very successful in the half-Iron/70.3-mile races, and riding and swimming with her, she looks quite strong.

We retired early to get to the starting line at six a.m. The morning will have us up before dawn to beat the heat as best we can. We will fight through the waves and the other competitors over 3.8 kilometres (2.4 miles) without a wetsuit for extra buoyancy. Like in Kona, the rules of triathlon state that when water temperatures exceed 24.5 degrees Celsius (76.1 Fahrenheit), the use of wetsuits is disallowed to prevent overheating. In these races, most racers wear swim skins, suits made from hydrophobic materials that reduce drag in the water. Water temperatures in Subic Bay on June 11 are expected to be 32 degrees Celsius (89.6 Fahrenheit). We will swim through seas as warm as bathwater to hit the beach running and get to our bikes as close as possible to an hour after the start.

I feel like even coming this far is miraculous. Even if I don't finish the race tomorrow, I will have achieved something just in building up my fitness to this point after two major breaks, three surgeries, and countless hours in intensive care in the past sixteen months. At the same time, it feels like losing my shot at the World Championships in Nice is a foregone conclusion. I don't think there's any way for me to get there. At the same time, having even come this far at my age is a worthy capstone to this story.

11 JUNE, 2023

Race day was a shocking whirlwind of events. I had prepped for the race thinking I would likely drop out midway, perhaps after the bike segment or at a convenient spot in the run. I was still not feeling 100 percent at the start, so I slipped my inhaler into my tri-suit. I knew having it in the back pocket of the suit might slow me down a little, but I figured it would be prudent to have it there. If I stopped breathing on the swim, I knew I would be done for. It's hard to recover from drowning, and safety is always at the forefront of my mind.

The water was warm and the skies slightly overcast as we lined up on the beach. It was a rolling start, but Steve and I started at the beginning, staying with the front of the age-group pack. I'm normally quite comfortable in the water, very in control of my breathing, but this time I just couldn't seem to get enough oxygen with each breath. I rolled onto my back about a kilometre into the swim and just lay there, floating in the warm ocean, holding onto the course rope, and staring up at the sky. Everything had slowed, and I remember thinking, *I really need to do something right now.* After a moment or so, I came to, reached for my inhaler, and took a puff. This snapped me back into focus. *Breathe. I need to breathe!* The oxygen deprivation was obviously doing some funny things to my head. I took a deep breath, took another, and then started toward the buoys again before the lifeguards could paddle over and try to convince me to get out of the water.

I had lost the front pack of swimmers but still hammered on stroke by stroke through the waves. I decided to push through despite my faltering position, rounded the second buoy, and then headed back to shore to complete the first lap. I took another puff on the inhaler and headed back out. The second lap was less eventful as I was swimming mostly on my own. I made it back to transition in one hour, sixteen minutes—one of the worst swim times I can remember in recent years—but I was still grateful I had the energy to keep going. For those counting, I had done an hour and three minutes last year in Kona.

I made it out of the water and thought, *Well, I got through the first part; now let's see what the bike is like.* In transition, I had racked a fair distance from Steve, so I had no idea where he was. Most likely he was already on the course hammering away on the bike. I got my swim skin off, put everything back in my transition bag, and then hit the bike course.

During the ride, it started raining on and off, which was a mercy. It dropped the temperature to around thirty degrees, much cooler than it had been. It also got a bit windy and wasn't too nice. About an hour from the finish, the skies opened up in a monsoon-like squall that drenched everyone on the course. I was forced to slow down as visibility dropped and the road surface went slick but managed to stay upright.

It was a four-lap bike course with quite a bit of climbing—almost 1,500 metres in total. After the first lap, I thought, *I can't keep doing this. I'm absolutely dead. That's only 40K down.* But then I thought to myself, or maybe the Mr. Hyde in me said, *Just get to the far end of the course.* By the time I got to the far end, I still wanted to quit but realised that I'd have to cycle 20km back to town to do so. It was all just psychology at this point, just talking myself into doing another lap and keeping the legs turning. This kept me going even through the squalls, knowing that I'd have to ride through them to get back to town no matter what I did.

Though I've commented before about how the bike has always been more dangerous to me than the other sports, a lot of cycling is just holding a decent cadence. This was no exception. I knew I wasn't going to be able to hold high watts or a fast pace, so instead I focused on getting as comfortable as possible in the aero tuck position, sitting low with my elbows in the padded cups and keeping weight off my wrist. I'd been able to get my bike position as aerodynamic as possible. On average, I was only burning 150 watts on the bike, but I hadn't lost much speed. I still needed to come out of the aero position from time to time to take another inhaler puff and make sure my lungs weren't closing up again but managed to avoid any trouble on this hot and humid course.

On each of the laps, the final ten kilometres was downhill, which was another blessing. It allowed me to recover a bit and forget the pain of the ascent just long enough to convince myself to take the next lap. I could just freewheel all the way back to town, passing people as I let myself roll down the descent. I came down the final hill into town having not pedalled for nearly ten minutes and checked my heart rate on my watch. It had gone down from 140 beats per minute on the inclines to just under 80. As I dismounted, I thought, *Maybe I can make it through this after all.*

Still stiff from holding that aero tuck for nearly six hours, I started to walk the course after racking my bike. I stretched and hobbled to get myself back onto the course, and after about fifteen minutes, I felt my legs start to loosen and come back. I started to slowly jog and then run the course.

At around ninety minutes in, around the twelve-kilometre mark, I suddenly felt my heart rate spike. I started getting short of breath and fell to my knees for a moment. I realised (thankfully quicker than the first time) that I was having another asthma attack and grabbed a few puffs on my inhaler again. From there, I started to just walk twenty steps, run twenty steps. Each time, I found I could go a little bit farther on the run, turning the feet over a few more times before I needed to take a break. After another kilometre, I found I was able to do a light jog over to the aid station and get some ice and a much-needed drink.

I decided I could jog to each of the aid stations, rest, and then jump back on the course. One of the great things about Ironman races is their volunteers. They're always happy to help out, and they're great at getting you exactly what you need. I'd get to one of these compact aid stations, struggling just to arrive each time, and I'd huff out requests as best I could. "Ice, please" and they'd hit me with a cup of ice. "Cola" and a cup of cola would almost immediately appear in my hand. Someone else would hand me a banana, a gel, or a salt tablet. I felt a bit like the driver of an F1 car in the pit stop. I'd arrive and these highly efficient volunteers would fall all over themselves to help me get back out on the course. A big 'hats off' to the race volunteers in Subic Bay who got me from aid station to aid station. They deserve quite a bit of gratitude.

I finally found with this strategy that I had gone from hitting ten minutes per kilometre down to six minutes. As I fuelled up and got a rhythm going, I saw the splits were starting to improve. For the last spell, I ended up doing about 5:35 per kilometre. I had started the run section of the race expecting a five-hour marathon but managed four hours and thirteen minutes. With my asthma attacks and weak leg, I couldn't get under four hours for the full forty-two kilometres, but it felt amazing to finish this race.

It turns out that I had finished the bike part of the race in second place in my age group. Steve had finished that section nearly thirty minutes ahead of me. As I was dealing with my asthma attacks, two racers from Korea passed me on the run. I was fortunately able to catch up to one of them during the last section of the race when I caught my final wind and eked out a third-place finish in a time of eleven hours and thirty-four minutes

This was good enough to qualify me for Nice. I had achieved what I set out to do even without needing to rely on the roll-down of spaces—after all my illnesses and strife. All in all, I'm feeling quite proud that just over a week ago I felt like I was at death's door but now have a qualifying spot for the World Championships. Steve won our age group in 11:19. I feel lucky we'll be able to travel together. Faith had a very strong race as well, taking first place in her age group in a very respectable 11:44. This was a successful day for the three of us, and celebration was in order.

The next key step for me is to recover from this properly and then start to rebuild. With twelve weeks to Nice, I should be able to pull back for a bit and then use the baseline I've built up to create some speed. I'll be back in Auckland with my family for a bit to get back on my feet again, but then I'll be off to France at the end of August to prepare for the race. Fingers crossed that the run-up to this race won't see any upsets to my preparation like bone breaks or pneumonia.

Claiming my qualification for the World Championship in Nice

Against all odds, I found my way to a World Championships spot. I will now be heading to Nice for the race in September. That will be the all-or-nothing moment: Either I take a podium spot after completing a best-of-the-best elite performance, or I retire from Iron-distance racing without a medal. In either case, I am heading into the race with high stakes and no remaining room for failure. Maybe this is where I can excel. In the past, I have pulled out some of my best performances when everything is down to the wire.

I can't help but wonder whether I might have bonked in a hot race like this if I had another option. I knew that barring a costly trip to Europe or the US, this was the last chance. In the end, I decided to go for it, and I felt sharp and on target. The combination of pressure and focus is what makes the sharpest tools so effective; a metal hammer and chisel can crack the perfect crystal lattice of a diamond when applied in the right way. I cracked this race and set myself up for my final Ironman, where I will vie for a podium slot against the best long-distance triathletes in the world.

Takeaways:

- **Learn to recognize fatigue and illness:**
  Earlier treatment of my illness might have had me feeling better by race day. By accepting the fact that I was not just tired and overheated but actively unwell, I could have had a much less nail-biting run-up to the race.
- **Listen to your body:**
  Rest days will happen whether you want them to or not; work too hard and your body will tell you when you need to take the time off. In hindsight, getting the proper rest I needed was what allowed me to finish the race. Listening to my body on the day, I also knew how hard I could possibly push through the brutally hot course.
- **It ain't over till it's over:**
  Even twenty-four hours before the starting gun, I wasn't sure I could make it to the race. I decided to go for it and leave behind no regrets.

The Last Valley

After Subic Bay, I needed several weeks to recover from both the illness and the effort of the race. My body had just about enough of the heat, and Steve and I were grateful to get back to the cooler climate of Auckland. There, my family helped me recover and build myself back up. As I've noted before, training makes you weaker, while rest and recovery are what allow you to become stronger. For a week after my return from the Philippines I let myself lie in, took our dog for short walks, and supported Rieko in her training as best I knew how.

Once my body had adequately recovered, I started back up gently, planning out a training schedule leading up to the championship race in Nice in September. I was back on the clock, but fortunately, I knew that my body had the baseline fitness to finish. The aerobic base was set simply by my finishing the race at the start of June. This meant that for the next eleven weeks, I could leverage that base to get my body into top form to not only finish the race but also to mount the podium.

Relaxation and downtime

Let's talk about the relaxation strategies that keep me sane amidst the whirlwind of training and competition. My secret weapons? Mindless entertainment and strategic self-care.

- *Emptying the Mind Before Bed:*
  When the training day is done, my brain tends to hum with residual energy. To switch it off, I find solace in the world of baking shows. The focus on precision and washes away the day's stresses. It's my mental bubble bath before drifting off to sleep.

- *Chess: A Mental Tonic:*

  Another way I unwind is by immersing myself in the logic and strategy of chess. A few games, even if they're against myself, are enough to quiet the chatter in my head and sharpen my focus. It's a mental massage, leaving me feeling refreshed and ready to tackle the next day.
- *Podcasts and Baking Shows: A Double Dose of Calm:*

  For times when my dyslexia makes reading a challenge, I turn to podcasts and audiobooks. They keep my mind engaged while I indulge in another favorite—those same baking shows! It's a double dose of relaxation, and I swear, the bakers' passion is contagious.
- *Acupuncture: My Pain-Relieving Ritual:*

  For physical relaxation, acupuncture is a godsend for me. My wife, an acupuncturist herself, works magic on my tired muscles and aching joints. It's like a targeted massage, relieving tension and boosting blood flow. Even today, when my Achilles starts to tighten, I know exactly where to turn for relief.
- *Prehab:*

  Speaking of preventing pain, I'm a big believer in prehab. Wearing compression socks even while I'm talking to you is just one way I stay ahead of the game. Whether it's stretching, strengthening exercises, or even the occasional ice bath, I'm constantly working to keep my body ready for whatever challenge comes next.
- *A Holistic Approach:*

  My relaxation strategies aren't just about quick fixes; they're part of a holistic approach to my well-being. They help me navigate the demands of training, recover from grueling races, and ultimately, keep my passion for triathlon and multisport burning bright.

My approach is a blend of mindful activities, strategic self-care, and a healthy dose of prehab. Remember, what works for me might not work for you. The key is to find what brings you peace and helps you unwind in a way that truly nourishes your mind and body.

Four-week speed-focused peak-phase training plan I used for Ironman 2023:

The following was my speed-focused set to help build muscular endurance and speed for the marathon at the end of the Ironman in Kona. I considered this to be a bit of a peak phase even though at the time I had barely come off the base build. It should be a doable set for anyone looking to build proper race speed off the bike, but it is not for the faint of heart!

Week	Day	Workout	Description	Effort
1	Monday	Off	Bike or Swim Focus Day	-
	Tuesday	Intervals	8 x 800m at 5K pace, 90-second jog recovery	8
	Wednesday	Easy Run	45 minutes easy, focus on recovery	4
	Thursday	Off	Swim Focus Day	-
	Friday	Tempo Run	20-minute warmup, 30 minutes at half-marathon pace, 10-minute cooldown	7
	Saturday	Long Run	90 minutes easy with 4 x 5-minute surges at 10K pace near the end (2-minute recovery)	6-7
	Sunday	Off	Bike Focus Day	-
2	Monday	Off	Swim or Bike Focus Day	-
	Tuesday	Hill Repeats	10 x 45-second uphill sprints, jog back recovery	8
	Wednesday	Easy Run	50 minutes easy, focus on recovery	4
	Thursday	Off	Bike Focus Day	-
	Friday	Progression Run	10-minute warmup, 40 minutes progressing from easy to 10K pace, 10-minute cooldown	6-8
	Saturday	Long Run	100 minutes steady, 10 minutes at marathon pace toward the end	6-7
	Sunday	Off	Swim Focus Day	-

3	Monday	Off	Bike or Swim Focus Day	-
	Tuesday	Intervals	6 x 1-mile at 10K pace, 2-minute jog recovery	8
	Wednesday	Easy Run	45 minutes recovery pace	4
	Thursday	Off	Bike Focus Day	-
	Friday	Tempo Run	15-minute warmup, 3 x 10 minutes at half-marathon pace with 5-minute recovery jog, 10-minute cooldown	7
	Saturday	Long Run	110 minutes easy with strides (8 x 20 seconds at 5K pace) in the final 20 minutes	6-7
	Sunday	Off	Swim Focus Day	-
4	Monday	Off	Swim or Bike Focus Day	-
	Tuesday	Intervals	10 x 400m at 3K pace, 90-second jog recovery	9
	Wednesday	Easy Run	40 minutes very easy, focus on recovery	3-4
	Thursday	Off	Bike Focus Day	-
	Friday	Tempo Run	20-minute warmup, 40 minutes at half-marathon pace, 10-minute cooldown	7
	Saturday	Long Run	120 minutes steady, last 20 minutes at marathon pace	6-7
	Sunday	Off	Swim Focus Day	-

Having built a fair bit of muscle and strength from training in the CrossFit gym that I had joined with Rieko was helpful in the recovery and restart of my training. Studies in exercise science have shown that we can take up to three weeks off before fitness begins to decline; the more muscle we have, the longer before the decline starts to set in. I took full advantage of this, letting my body quit itself of the pneumonia and fatigue before commencing the next phase of my plan.

Steve and I regularly met up for ocean swims, bike rides, and runs, and encouragement from my friends at the gym remained crucial to getting me back out. As I have noted, I am a social person by nature and appreciate the camaraderie of working with other people. Many distance athletes note the difficulties with loneliness on long runs or rides, and I know that I perform at my best when I have a pack to run or cycle with. Though I do a fair bit of training on my own, and a lot of my recovery was spent working through the necessary exercises all by my lonesome, it was the desire to get back out and spend time on the roads and trails with friends and family that got me to push through the pain of every stretch, every mobility session, every agonizing step of rehab.

These connections brought me back to Japan in July and August of 2023. I came back both to see important friends and family and also to rebuild my heat adaptation for Nice. Both Japan and southern France are known for their heat and humidity during the summer months, so training with my old comrades at the Japan Triathlon Union, Triathlon in Tokyo, and Namban Rengo would be a boost for both body and spirit.

During this period, the daily high could get close to forty degrees (104F) with miserably high humidity above eighty percent on some days, meaning that anything we did out of the water needed to get done right at dawn to prevent heat exhaustion. Long rides started early in the day, sometimes before dawn. Even before sunrise, there were days when I would start out on a ride or run only to be dripping with sweat after only fifteen minutes on the road. At the same time, I realised after my pneumonia in Indonesia and feeling that every day was a struggle wasn't me or my lack of fitness. Now, without the fevers brought on by illness, I was able to cope with the heat as well as any of the locals. This heat adaptation was crucial for me in getting ready for Nice, which promised to have equally blistering temperatures.

One important event during my stay in Japan was a memorial for a friend, Otsuka Toru, who passed away in 2023. It was quite sudden and unexpected, and I was sorry to be forced to say a final goodbye so soon.

He had been a training partner, a rival, and an excellent racer back in the 1990s. We had trained together nearly every day for ten years when I was younger. He had maintained his fitness even after leaving the pro circuit.

Otsuka-san trained with a strong squad of young and up-and-coming racers who are still chasing records around Japan today. I met with his team, and we were able to go for a long ride, pushing up and down the mountains in Ibaraki, north of Tokyo. I organized everything as a memorial for him, going over some of the courses we used to do. It was a good experience for all. For me, I was able to chase down some young bucks with a competitive fire, keeping them going, and for them I was able to show that life after a pro career doesn't have to mean the end of training and racing. In leading them up and down the mountains, I showed them the titanium mindset—don't let yourself rust, and learn to recover well enough that you can always do the next set, the next session, the next block of training. For me, though, I wasn't always the fastest one out there with everyone; it was about getting out and trying to do a little more, going a little harder, and keeping that going as long as I could. It was an honour to be able to share this with training partners old and new.

The run home

It was 1989, and my running form was going to be gracing the pages of a new English language textbook published by a famous university press. After my time in Japan and my growing success as a professional triathlete, the publisher wanted me and my story to be used as a model and example for English learners, providing an interesting example of the applications of the language. Working with the publisher meant a nice night out with some of the writers and marketing representatives from the corporate side. They whisked me away for a celebratory dinner, offering me a chance to talk in depth over a nice meal.

I had planned to be on my best behavior. They, however, had other ideas. Beers flowed, replaced by whiskeys, and soon, I was their designated tipsy entertainment. It seems they thought it might be fun to see how well an athlete could hold his liquor, but my ability to drink surprised them. Little did they know, and as I've mentioned before, I used to be a bit of a party animal in my younger days. Anyone who knows Japan will know that many athletes there know how to handle the rounds as well—work hard, play hard, as they say. Even though I had reduced my drinking from my university days, I guess my body remembered how to process that volume of alcohol—practice makes permanent, after all. No matter how many drinks they poured, I managed to keep myself upright.

Finally, they called it a night and handed me a £50 note to catch a taxi home. After I said goodbye, I looked at the note, checked my watch, and looked down the road. I hadn't done much of a run that day, so I thought, *Why not?* I tightened up the laces of my dress flats (no sneakers for a night out), checked my watch, and I was off toward home.

Getting home in a straight line that evening meant taking the A1 motorway. In retrospect, it's a wonder I didn't end up dead on the side of the road as cars whizzed by at seventy miles per hour in the dark, but I was young, drunk, and feeling pretty fit.

The miles melted away as I hit my stride. Perhaps it was the alcohol and the high from the enjoyment of the evening, but that was one of the easiest runs I can remember. I sobered up just enough midway along to realize that my non-athletic shoes weren't getting the traction I was used to, but I shrugged it off as soon as I realized there was nothing to be done. Soon, I was at my doorstep.

When I walked in, my housemate was surprised. "You're awfully sweaty. And earlier than we expected."

"I took the A1 home."

"But haven't you been drinking? Do you mean you took a cab? We didn't hear a car pull up."

"I ran the whole way."

My housemates were speechless. I tapped my watch, "And I made it in an hour." I had held a six-minute-mile pace (~3:45/km) the whole way back while drunk and in business shoes. The story of that night became a running (pardon the pun) joke amongst friends. The £50 note the book reps had given me for taxi fare found its way into my pocket, a trophy for my secret midnight dash. This was just a little bit of textbook-worthy mischief, but sometimes we win by doing things that are a bit outside and above common expectations.

All in all, during my stay I was able to get in about 20 kilometres (~12 miles) of open-water swimming, 1,000 kilometres (~600 miles) on the bike, and 100 kilometres (~60 miles) of running in just over two weeks. With thirty-plus hours of training each week, I still felt the desire to take a day off here or there to stay in bed or avoid the heat in a nice air-conditioned room. To get through this, I reminded myself about my dear friend who had just passed. He no longer had the option to train, so it was almost my duty to keep going, knowing that he would have still been out there in the heat if he could.

Once my time in Japan was finished, it was time to head to Nice to get ready for the race. I once again packed my bike in a sturdy cardboard box with plenty of padding and flew across the world. In France, I once again met up with Steve Farrell and Alistair Adams to prepare for the race, just as we had done the previous October.

We booked a small apartment just 100 metres from the Mediterranean. When I say small, I do mean it; there was one room, a pullout sofa bed, and a single bed in the corner, with a washroom and kitchen and not much else. To be honest, it again reminded me of student life, sharing rooms and bunking with friends. We drew lots again, and it came out once more that Ali and I would share the sofa bed. As always, our wives gave us a bit of grief about it being "that kind of mates trip," but we took the teasing in stride and were grateful to have a bed to crash in after the long days under the sun. More than this, we had been burned the previous year by the unscrupulous rental owners cancelling on us and then doubling the price due to the demand for hotels, and we wanted to make sure no one would swipe the rug out from under us again. We chose the most 'utilitarian' option that we could find that would also accommodate the three of us and our bikes.

The bonus for us being packed in tight as sardines was not only being close to the beach but also to the cafes and restaurants by the seafront. The location was gorgeous, and from where we were sitting, this was far and away better than going to Hawaii. While Kona has the history and origin story of the Ironman behind it, this location was far and away better than what we had experienced the previous year. A number of well-known people had complained quite loudly about the decision to split the men's and women's races and move them to new locations. From the food prices to the cost of travel from anywhere in Europe, my mates and I would fall squarely on the opposite side of these critics. Nice is a

fantastic location for a race, in many ways superior to Kona.

Our preparation for the race included daily swims in the warm waters of the Mediterranean, bike reconnaissance along the course, and runs up and down the beach. With my leg now fully healed and without any additional attachments to keep it in place, I felt more comfortable and confident during the bike and run portions. Having lost several hundred grams of metal and returning my muscles to their pre-accident positioning (rather than working around a foreign object), I could feel my body's relief. It felt a bit like taking off a heavy backpack and then trying to run again. My hips opened up and mobility had definitely returned, so the main problem now was simply lack of power. That right leg continued to underperform, and it would take quite a bit more time before I was anywhere close to balanced.

After my hot and heavy training block in Japan, I felt confident that I could hold somewhere in the range of 160 to 200 watts for the full 180 kilometres of the Ironman course. While this still wasn't anywhere near the power I used to be comfortable putting out, I knew it would be enough to get me near the top. I was relying on the run a bit for my projections of a decent finishing time, aiming to hit somewhere in the range between 3:30 and 3:45 total time for the marathon.

Now, though the legs were mostly healed, the wrist was still problematic. At the same time, I decided I wasn't going to focus on it. I could make excuses all day as to why my swim wasn't better or why riding on my wrists for hours wasn't going to be an option, but that wouldn't make me go any faster on race day. The pain was always going to be there and always going to be a problem so long as I had the pins holding the bones together. The pain wasn't going to be enough to stop me from finishing this race.

One issue that had started to come up now was that my left foot had started to cramp. The issue seemed to be that relying on the left leg to compensate for the weaknesses in the right had caused minor overuse injuries all up and down the leg. As I would run, swelling would pinch the nerves, and I would start to get involuntary cramps in that left foot. I had been playing with different shoes, shoe sizes, and inserts, but none of them really solved the issue. I could finish the first half of the marathon

On the road to Nice

without problems, and on a good day I would only cramp once or twice toward the end of the second half, but on a bad day, I would just have to grin and bear it to the end.

I never spoke of this previously, but I now wonder if I could have finished the Ironman race in Subic Bay after my bout of pneumonia with the rods in my thigh. Though unconnected to the lungs directly, when I had the rods in I could still feel the movement of the muscle around the titanium contraption that held my femur together for nearly a year. In times of extreme duress, like a race, with my whole body on fire from the lactic burn, I stopped feeling the specific pain in the leg, but its influence was unmistakable. Had I been competing with decreased oxygen capacity from the pneumonia, and with the pins in the leg demanding more of my body's resources to compensate for their weight and the offset in my muscles, I fear that race might have gone differently and this story might not have led to training in France. Instead, I would have metaphorically hung up my Ironman shoes.

I have never aimed to be forever competing at the ultradistances. My goal from the start was to get on the podium at the World Championships, simply to prove that as a sixty-year-old man, I could. Before the accident, I dreamed of taking the top place at Kona and now in Nice, but I have always felt much happier and more comfortable at the shorter distance races—5K runs, 10K runs, half-marathons, sprint triathlons, even Olympic-distance and half-Ironman events. In seeking a place at the top, I was seeking to prove that it was possible to get there; first to myself as I grew older and then to the world after my accident. Either way, this dream had already taken a year longer than I had planned, and I was starting to itch for the more familiar territory of short-course races. No matter the outcome, Nice would be my final full Ironman race.

With all the training and preparation, it is easy to forget that the most important parts of our lives happen outside of sport. While training for me has probably added years to my life and has certainly added life to my years, my family and friendships have always been the fire that keeps me going. As I've noted many times here, the people around me have always gotten me through the hard workouts and most painful moments. While there are relatively small life events that I have missed for training and races, I have always been fortunate enough to be able to prioritise friends and family when they needed me most.

However, the opposition of these two worlds came to a head in the weekend just before the race. One of my closest friends, one of the best people in my life for many years, was in a serious accident back in England. I immediately dropped everything to go back and be with them in their time of need and help ensure that everything went smoothly. Fortunately, Nice is just a short flight from London, and I was able to get a seat on the next flight. In that moment, I seriously considered abandoning the race.

Had this been any other time of any other year, I would have been half a world away. From Auckland, Hawaii, or Tokyo, I don't think I could have gotten to the UK in less than twenty-four hours at the fastest, and I might have had to get another mortgage on my house to pay for that ticket. Being camped out in the south of France, I was able to get to the UK hospital less than four hours after I received the terrible news. I arrived to find everyone gathered about and worried, but I had missed the worst part of the waiting. I was fortunate to arrive to find they were in stable condition and being well cared for by family and friends. It was honestly like a movie scene, arriving in the hospital after hearing the worst to find so many people I care about gathered, and then to be able to hug them all as we cried tears of relief.

My friend was clearly still in bad shape, but once we were able to talk, they were touched that I had come so quickly. Moments like this and the loss of my friend and training partner during the summer reminded me just how short and precious life can be. During this brief interlude, I could see what truly mattered and that win or lose, finish or don't, the people in my life would always come first. With my friend stable and well cared for, I was able to head back to Nice by the middle of the week to prepare for the race that following Sunday. I resolved to take my friend's blessing and well-wishes and convert that into fuel for the quite literally long road ahead of me.

Takeaway:

- **Friends and family first:**
  Be ready to abandon fitness dreams when the bigger picture becomes clearer. Family and friends are just as important to our survival as our goals and dreams. Keep them safe and healthy.

Ironman World Championships: Nice 2023

My friend's illness reminded me that the people in my life will always come before any race, no matter how significant. As I mentioned, this was a tough time for me to get away, but I was fortunate that I could book a flight to London from southern France immediately and get there within the day. Thankfully, my friend was recovering, and with their blessing, I crossed the channel again to complete my journey. I was back in Nice, but those three days in London, filled with stress and sleepless nights, had taken a toll. My back ached, and the adrenaline rush of worrying about my friend had worn off. Now I was down to the race, and the uncertainty of the past two years was finally creeping up on me.

Normally a good sleeper (see Relaxation and Downtime in the previous chapter"), I found that I was plagued by a restless mind. Would I wake up on race day ready to conquer? Might I start off strong only to burn out and find myself struggling? Would I even finish? Prior races had been good for me, giving me a goal to overcome. Here I was steps from the summit, and I was wracked with doubts. I knew how to pace myself, and I knew that my preparation was done, but I still found myself troubled in the final nights before I had to step onto the course.

The process of preparing for this race helped me regain my health not once, not twice, but three times now—first with my leg, then my arm, then with pneumonia. The motivation to get back to feeling fit and staying there wasn't just for the race; it was for my friends and, most importantly, my family. I wanted to be there for them as long as I could. I realised that this back-and-forth was likely why my mind was so ill at ease. I had worked myself back to physical fitness, had continued to provide for my family through the buildup of my coaching business, and had done everything I could to take care of my friends, colleagues, and clients, but sudden events and illnesses can blindside any of us.

People often talk about luck, but I see it differently. I mended a broken leg, recovered from a fractured arm, and raced through pneumonia. Each challenge made me stronger. I felt fortunate to be able to help my friend when they needed me despite being able to do very little except show up. Fitness has always been my ally, making life's hurdles a bit easier to clear. As a racer, most of the obstacles I face are primarily issues of distance and time—all I'm ever doing is getting from one place to another as fast as I possibly can. I did this for my friend, and now I was going to do it once more. Despite the uncertainty, I knew I'd get through it, one way or another. As soon as I had resolved that in my mind, I was finally able to sleep properly.

My family and friends around me were my support team. Steve was there, checking the course and keeping me grounded. My son Tommy had flown back with me from London to provide support and a bit more social media coverage for our growing coaching business. As I said, I don't really believe in luck, but I do believe in gratitude, and by this measure, I had much to be thankful for.

Race day arrived, and it felt like a blessing. At this point in the story, you've heard enough about race preparation and the details of everything that goes into an Ironman. I'll spare you those details except to say that I was ready to hit the course. We would be jumping into the Mediterranean in a mass start in the morning, heading out into the mountains around Nice on the bike, and then running the flat roads along the beaches to look out over the sea. The course promised to be idyllic, at least matching the iconic Kona course and in many ways offering more scenic views.

The swim went spectacularly well. I emerged in the lead group, just thirty seconds off the front, one of my best swims in a long time. I felt confident, ready to tackle the rest of the day. Steve came out of the water seconds ahead of me, and we both headed into the bike area together, stripping off our swimskins and getting ready for six hours of pedalling. Grabbing my bike and heading to the course, I found myself ahead of

Steve due to a minor mishap he had with his gear. I knew I'd see him again soon and we'd be working our way around the course as close together as the drafting rules might allow. I started the bike leg strong, perhaps a bit too strong given my condition.

The bike course was brutal—2,500 metres of climbing under the relentless Mediterranean sun. The weeks I had spent in Japan, famously more hot and humid than New Orleans in the summer, worked in my favour. I knew my heat adaptation was good, and I pushed hard, again perhaps too hard. Eventually, the heat began to take its toll. Dehydration and cramps set in, primarily in my right leg. The rods removed from my leg in March had left it slightly weaker than before, and I still hadn't fully recovered the strength in some of the smaller thigh muscles around my knee and hip. I could feel them clenching and failing to unclench, but I grabbed another salt tab, downed the last of my sports drink, and pushed through. I made it back to transition coasting downhill for nearly thirty kilometres. The downhill was a blessed respite for my legs, and I used every bit of my downhill ability to take each switchback at the fastest and safest speed possible. Getting to see beautiful countryside while the wind from the descent cooled my overheating body reminded me why I continue to race and raised my spirits as I headed back to the coast for the transition.

I emerged from transition to find Tommy waiting for me and cheering. "You're in second place, Dad!" he shouted as I got my shaky legs turning. "The next guy is thirty seconds behind you!" The pressure was on. Starting the run, the heat hit me like a wall. The first lap of the four-lap course was okay, but the cramps I had started to develop on the bike were a constant threat. My calves and thighs contracted completely around the twenty-kilometre mark. My leg would seize up entirely, forcing me to stop and stretch. Tommy, acting as support, was running up and down along the sidelines, keeping me updated on my position. "You've dropped to third, but the next guy is still a few minutes behind," Tommy called out. "You've just got to hold this pace!"

Unfortunately, that would prove an impossibility. With five kilometres to go, I found myself in a desperate shuffle trying to keep the cramps at bay. A U-turn at the five-kilometre mark triggered a severe cramp, forcing me to stop and stretch against a fence. I knew I had five minutes to spare, but my leg refused to cooperate. I walked to the aid station under the blazing sun, drank some water and cola, grabbed a banana,

Taking a moment just shy of the finish

and managed to get on my way. *Just a bit more to go,* I told myself. Tommy had seemingly run a full marathon himself while jogging up and down the sidelines to give me updates. "The fourth-place guy is just two minutes behind you. Now is the time to turn those legs!" Despite his encouragement, with just one kilometre to go, I hit the wall. The cramps were unbearable, and I collapsed on the grass at the side of the road. Spectators encouraged me, but my body had reached its limit. Tommy caught up and saw me at my low point, snapping photos of my cramping legs. He bent down and whispered, "Dad, it's less than a kilometre to the finish. You got this; you just gotta give a bit more."

I knew he was serious because that was when he stopped giving me reports on my place in the race. I had lost my third-place spot, but I knew I could still make the podium with a top-five finish. I summoned my courage, did a final stretch to get the legs going, and let the foam and carbon plates in my shoes do their magic and roll me the final steps to the finish line. As a runner, I have poked fun at the look of race walkers over the years, but no more. I was more or less copying their form as I tried to keep my body from clenching up tight with the fatigue and lack of minerals. Less than a minute behind the man who had passed me, I crossed the finish line fourth in my age group with a time of eleven hours, seventeen minutes, six seconds.

While this time was indeed slower than my time the year before, the tough elevation gains on the bike made course comparisons impossible. With any race, we race the course and the people around us, and we cannot compare results from one course to another with any reliability. Even though my overall time was slower, I felt better about my performance this time. I knew that I had truly given my all.

This experience taught me that when the body shuts down, it shuts down. While I have had several tough races, some of the toughest within the past few years, this one was notable for how close I came to reaching my absolute limit before reaching the finish line. Despite the disappointment of not being able to take home the crown, finishing in the top five and making it to the podium was a victory in itself. Reflecting on the journey, I realised that getting the rods removed from my leg had very much impacted my performance, but it was necessary for my long-term health.

While I had a tough day, Steve came back an absolute wreck. Just ahead of me on the swim and a bit behind on the bike, he finished several hours after me on the run. While I had tried to run as much as I could, Steve brought his own persistent injuries to the race, and they brought him to a walking pace on that blisteringly hot day. I saw him come in three hours after me, having finished the run leg in over six-and-a-half hours, which was longer than it took him to finish the 180km on the bike. This is a further testament to the fact that no matter how tough, how fit, and how well-trained you are, when the body says no, it will say it in no uncertain terms. My mate is still a hero for not giving up, though I was very lucky to have him at my back the whole way—or I wouldn't have nailed fourth place!

Reflecting on the course, Nice was phenomenal. In many ways, it's a more exciting venue than Kona. Swimming in the Mediterranean is just as nice as swimming in Hawaii, and perhaps better due to the lack of volcanic rocks. The bike course demanded skill and effort. It was a true test of an athlete's ability. Drafting wasn't an issue; the climbs and technical sections required individual effort. The run by the seaside was fairly flat and offered some stunning views out over the Mediterranean, though I will admit that I did not enjoy them as much as in the days just before and after the race. By the third lap, I was longing to dip myself in the inviting waters. In the debate on the rotating venue for the Ironman World Championships, I find myself firmly in the camp supporting the decision to move. A change of scenery, a challenging course, and a beautiful location had all been lined up, and the race organization was top-notch as always. Even after my frustrations and difficulties in the months before while figuring out the races I needed to do to qualify, I am quite satisfied with my experience racing under the Ironman banner.

Despite the challenges, I was thrilled with my performance. Completing the race after such a tumultuous week was an accomplishment in itself. Compounded with everything I had come through, I felt vindicated knowing that I could bounce back from just about anything—after all, I had just done what others told me was nearly impossible.

As I have said many times, this puts a bow on this chapter of my life and closes this book, but it is not the final chapter in the story by any means. As a competitor, I knew I had to get back out there and aim for the next target, and I was already on my way. As we closed up our rental property in Nice, I was preparing for the next chapter in Spain. In two weeks, I would be competing in the Age Group World Championship super-sprint triathlon in Spain, shifting from doing one of the longest possible races to the shortest.

Takeaway:

- **When you reach your true limit, you'll know:** There are times when your body will just shut down, and these are the hard limits. Train so you never hit that point during a race.
- **The differences are as important as the similarities:** Compare efforts and achievements, but recognize that the same distance race on a different course will present a completely different set of experiences.

11

Back on Top

In the weeks following my Ironman race, I participated in two more major races. I had qualified for the super-sprint championships under the governance of the World Triathlon Union, the same group that oversees the Olympic and Paralympic triathlons. The race took place in Pontevedra, Spain. I represented New Zealand in both the Olympic/standard-distance race (1.5km swim, 40km bike, 10km run) and the super-sprint race (300m swim, 6.4km bike, 1.6km run). Steve Farrell, my constant traveling companion over the past few months, joined me for this adventure as well. It was only a short jaunt from Nice to head down the coast and across the border into Spain, another fortunate feature of the timing and location of the Ironman World Championships.

For many people I talked to, the reaction was the same: *Such a short race must be easy for you now that you've competed in so many Ironman races!* To them, I always told them the same thing: "It's a shorter race, but you suffer just as much!" As noted many times in this book, the longer races are about developing the discipline to suffer at a moderately high level for a very long time. These shorter races are all about how well you can suffer at a very high level for a relatively short time.

The Saturday on race weekend was the super-sprint race. I came out of the water with a healthy lead of several seconds, but somehow during my setup of the transition area, I had failed to securely place my helmet on my bike. It had somehow been knocked off, so I had to grab it off the ground. To make matters worse, it appeared that someone had stepped on the plastic buckle as they passed by, making it unusable! I had to fumble in transition, losing more than thirty seconds securing the two ends of the buckle in a *mostly* rules-acceptable fashion before heading back out onto the course. This rookie mistake on my part decided the race. Though I stuck with the lead pack until the very end, the top three finishers (Steve among them) had grabbed a lead I couldn't make up. I watched the three of them cross the finish line metres ahead of me while I was pushing on the final sprint.

I managed to get the buckle repaired but vowed not to make the same mistake the next day at the standard-distance race. This time I set up the transition area properly and secured my helmet in a way that it couldn't get knocked or blown about. I had another strong swim, coming in first after 1,500 metres in the water. I hit the bike as hard I could, holding my lead for the 40km, then donning my shoes for the run.

A challenger wearing an American flag on his bib caught me on the run, and we were stride for stride until the finish. I had thought I could beat him on the final sprint, so I held back to save energy, matching his pace as we went. He was obviously following my strategy—and maybe following what I teach in my Instagram posts! He held on until the end, putting up a powerful kick at the end. I tried to match him but could feel the fatigue from both the sprint and the Ironman as I tried to get just a bit more power out of my right leg, but he took the victory from me by one second. It was another disappointing day, but as I poured water over myself to cool down from my effort under the Spanish sun, I reflected on my journey to get there.

Like the water washing away the perspiration and heat, the sting of defeat subsided as I considered all I had accomplished. *A top-five finish at three different distances is something to be proud of, but there's still more work to be done.* After all I had come through—the agony of two major breaks, surgeries, and recoveries in eighteen months—I remained determined not to let this be the end.

Several weeks later, I arrived in Phu Quoc, Vietnam with a mix of excitement and trepidation. I had registered for the Ironman 70.3 race, sometimes called a Half-Ironman. As might be expected, all of the distances of an Ironman race are halved: 1.9km swim, 90km bike, 21.1km (half-marathon) run. I had recovered from my races in Europe and the subsequent jet lag getting back to New Zealand. Now I was aiming at one last long-distance race to test myself.

Race day arrived with a brilliant sunrise, casting a golden hue over the island. The swim start was as chaotic as I expected. Bodies churned the water into a frothy mess, and it was a fight to find space and rhythm. The saltwater burned my throat and eyes, but I pushed through, focusing on my stroke and breathing. Emerging from the water, I glanced at my watch—37:08. Not bad, but the real challenge was just beginning.

Transitioning to the bike, the heat was already building. The bike course was punishing: long stretches of rough road, unrelenting hills, and the ever-present Southeast Asian sun. I settled into a rhythm, concentrating on my nutrition plan. Electrolytes, water, gels—each one a crucial part of my strategy to keep going. The kilometres ticked by slowly, each one a victory over the elements. By the time I finished the 90km bike leg in 2:45:17, I was already exhausted, but I knew I could hammer out a half-marathon.

The run was where the real test of endurance began. The heat was suffocating, and the humidity made every breath an effort. My legs felt heavy, and my energy was waning. But I had trained for this. I had pushed through similar conditions in training and in my previous races, and I knew I could do it again. The Mediterranean heat in September had prepared me for this, and my body still remembered how to perform in these conditions. One step at a time, one kilometre at a time. I poured water over my head, took in salt tablets, and kept moving. The finish line came into view, and with it, a surge of energy. I crossed it in 1:44:01, completely spent but victorious. I claimed the top spot on the podium that day for men over sixty, at last showing how a titanium man can bounce back to full strength.

A careful reader will note that this was the first truly major victory of mine that I've described since the start of this book; the other races included a qualifying race, a podium finish, or a commendation for simply completing in whatever bedraggled condition I was in at the starting line, but chasing gold remained elusive. Finally winning my age group was a triumph, but more importantly, it was proof of my resilience and determination. All people have the capacity to bounce back from life's upsets, big and small. We are all titans, made of the sternest and most resilient materials, and we can recover with a combination of good science, strong will, and consistency. Coming to this moment a year and a half after all my illnesses and injuries, I had faced the hospitals, the heat, the hills, the humidity, and I had conquered all.

Is this the end of the book or just the end of this chapter?

I've said several times now that the Ironman chapter of my life has finished; I never need to do another full Iron-distance race. The sprint and Olympic-distance races have shown me that even though I'm not the fastest Ironman competitor in the world for my age group, I can still rank at the top across all triathlon distances with hard work and discipline. This to me is another mark of being a titanium-level athlete. As noted several times in this book, titanium is versatile and flexible. At the same time, it retains its base shape. It wants to return to the way it was set. I have always been most comfortable at shorter-distance endurance races; the suffering is sharper, the finish quicker, and the training suits my temperament. Moving forward, I will be working on maintaining endurance, speed, strength, flexibility, and balance as I age while helping my clients and followers do the same.

As I've been working on this book and talking to people, one comment that often comes up is the idea that I can do these things because I'm somehow a natural athlete who can bounce back from any setback to come out on top. I won't deny that I have had some excellent luck along the way, quite a bit of it from my parents. At the same time, the genetic lottery is really only half of the equation. The training is just as important, and while I've achieved the best things I can with the body I have, it's always been my mission to help others achieve what they can with the bodies they were given.

In this spirit, I'd like to take this moment to highlight how the weeks surrounding the Pontevedra races in 2023 went for the other people appearing in this book. They have been following the same sports science and using my coaching and advice to achieve steady incremental gains that have led to some inspiring results.

- My constant training partner, Steve Farrell, was able to take second in the super-sprint and fifth in the Olympic-distance race—the mirror opposites of my fifth place in the super-sprint and second at the Olympic distance. He was coming off injuries and all of the aches and pains of the Ironman in Nice just like me and managed a similarly impressive showing. He's been there doing my workouts week in, week out.
- My son, Tommy, ran a personal best of 33:05 for a 10K. He's been constantly building his fitness and his team of athletes to perform to the best of their abilities. Following our training plans, walking the walk, he showed that these plans lead to results primarily through dedication. The people he's coaching are all showing similar benefits to their health, and this spreads into well-being in the rest of their lives as well. He helped me craft the plans I used that I've detailed throughout this book.
- In 2025, Tommy went on to get his name entered in the Guiness Book of World Records for the Fastest Marathon while wearing Crocs. He clocked a time of 2:48:48—a very fast marathon in and of itself, but he managed to do it while wearing absolutely ridiculous pink footwear.
- Callum Elson, one of our NRG coaches, demonstrated the absolute precision that the racing discipline requires. He competed at the World Athletics Road Running Championships in Riga, Latvia, running a personal best in the one-mile road race in 3:56.41. Coming in second place, he finished .28 seconds behind the new world record holder and .03 seconds in front of the bronze-medal finisher. This race shows the incredible exactness required to compete at the top. If you watch the video of the final break, a hair's difference in either direction for any of the competitors could have meant victory, a world record, or a fourth-place finish. Callum proved his mettle, and we can expect great things going forward.
- Quint, the coauthor of this book, got his sprint triathlon time down to 1:05, a personal best. He secured the title of champion in his age group across Japan for the second consecutive year in 2023, and like me has since gone on to expand toward other forms of hybrid racing.
- My frequent podcast collaborator Darren Lakes ran under 1:22 at the Sydney Half Marathon. He used a negative-split strategy, showing discipline and keeping his pace just right, then gradually speeding up in the second half of the race. Discipline not just in training but also on race day can pay some impressive dividends.

- Note: Unlike Steve and Callum, Quint and Darren have never been professional athletes; they also don't have my genetics. They just follow the workout plans, work them into their busy work and family schedules, and grind out each session as best they can. While they haven't broken any world records, their achievements are a testament to how high you can go as a dedicated age grouper, and they make fine training partners.
- Last but hardly least, my wife Rieko competed in a 100-kilometre trail race in Tarawera, New Zealand, finishing in an astonishing time of thirteen hours, forty-five minutes. It was a testament to not only her strength and spirit but also the stellar patience and planning skills needed to compete in a gruelling event of this nature: running in the dark over obstacles on unfamiliar trails with little guidance or support beyond what you can carry yourself. Since then, she has competed in the Hyrox games in Sydney and Auckland and took gold and bronze respectively for her age group. She has followed a punishing training regimen to get her there, and it should not be forgotten how she's built her own incredible fitness while supporting me through my own recovery. Just as she has been there for me the whole way, I have done everything I can to support her performances as well.

I'm certain I've left out several noteworthy performances that other people surrounding me turned in around that time; please forgive me for this. I described the accomplishments of the others to make it clear that the hard work and smart training that went into my story of recovery are not fluke events or somehow special to me. I believe that everyone can achieve their best with a well-informed and science-based foundation for their training, and I share my story here as an example of how to do that.

To this end, two days after my race in Pontevedra, I was back to coaching. I conducted several clinics with my colleagues and friends at the Running Room in London. I wanted to help their runners get to the next personal best just as my own collaborators and clients have. We worked through many of the drills I have noted in this book that helped me literally get back to walking and then running on my own two feet. By the end of the sessions, I saw excellent progress. As a teacher and coach, it's massively gratifying to watch success begin to take hold before my eyes.

The sessions at the Running Room had an added benefit for me. I was able to do a force-plate analysis using all of the latest metrics that they set up. I learned that my ideas about running can be constantly challenged even after competing for half a century. I had always believed that my most effective cadence was 180 steps per minute—all the best science had pointed in that direction. Instead, I learned that I was likely going to be most efficient at 197 steps per minute. I used these insights when running my race in Phu Quoc.

Even now, after closing the door on Ironman, I'm using sports science to look forward to next year. I have new goals—teach my body to go fast again and build the strength and endurance needed to take the top spot in my age group in hybrid races like Hyrox. I'll be using every weapon in my training arsenal to get there as I run off toward the future and have as much fun as I can along the way. I appreciate your endurance coming through this journey with me. I wish you all the best so that you too can apply titanium-solid principles to your life and training.

Takeaway:

- **Celebrate your achievements, no matter how small they seem:**
  Even if you don't achieve all of your goals, it's important to recognize and appreciate the progress you've made. Every step forward is a victory.
- **Celebrate others' achievements:**
  We all are working hard to get ahead as best we can, and there's no loss in celebrating when others win, even when they come from a competitor. Every win deserves recognition.
- **There's always another race, another chance to improve and grow:**
  Don't dwell on past disappointments. Focus on the future and the opportunities that lay ahead.
- **The journey is just as important as the destination:**
  The experiences you gain and the lessons you learn along the way are invaluable even if you don't reach your ultimate goal.
- **Give yourself permission to move on when the time is right:**
  It's okay to step back from a challenge or goal if it no longer serves you. There's no shame in recognizing when it's time to move on to something new.

Epilogue

My story, like all stories, won't be over until I'm gone. I'm certain that even if I'm confined to a bed for the rest of my life, I'll be setting goals for how to achieve grandmaster status as a chess player. As I've tried to show through these stories and recollections, I'm not one to give up; I'm a survivor. I have been fortunate that none of my injuries has left me permanently incapacitated, but looking at the stories of other survivors, I am certain I would be among the ranks of those who bounced back. While others have overcome even greater obstacles, my goal in telling these stories is to show what is possible with hard work and determination.

Nothing about what I've done is special. While I certainly have had some advantages in my life, I've had just as many obstacles placed in my path (some of them placed there by none other than yours truly). In many ways, I feel like I've wasted my talents. If I'd only given that last ten percent when I was young rather than having fun with my friends or chasing women, I might have achieved greater heights. I will always have regrets for what could have been. At the same time, I know that those regrets are illusions. The difference for me is that I try not to carry my regrets around. For me, the secret to true resilience is to put down those regrets and disappointments of the past and focus on the future. For anyone seeking to recover after a setback, to bounce back stronger like titanium, we have to first set down all of the weight that was causing us to bend and buckle in the first place.

I'm now close to an age that used to be when mandatory retirements set in. After that, people were officially senior citizens, entitled to a pension, a spot on a park bench, and a discount on public transport. While I don't want to think of myself as that old, the truth of the matter is that age will catch up with me, and I will start slowing down. The question

is simply one of how much and how fast.

In the summer of 2024, I had another health scare. I was diagnosed with atherosclerosis, a hardening and partial obstruction of three of my major arteries. Though I have generally enjoyed a clean lifestyle—avoiding red meat, never smoking, and drinking only socially for most of my adult life—this condition crept up on me at the age of sixty-two, and I was required to go in for exploratory surgery to discover the extent of the obstructions. My doctors, some of the best in New Zealand, informed me that these arteries are nearly sixty percent blocked! It seems that this genetic condition had been waiting to pounce for some time. It was only thanks to generally good health habits and regular exercise that I'd managed to hold it off for this long.

Needless to say, this came as unwelcome news. I was told I would need to stay below my maximum heart rate as much as possible when racing. Fortunately, I developed a very strong heart over the years, and as I have discussed in several of the race reports, I know I can keep my heart rate low and still race well.

Though my top aerobic and anaerobic thresholds have diminished, I am still able to compete and set new goals. I travelled to Torremolinos, Spain for the Age Group World Championships triathlon in 2024 and competed there again in the sprint and standard-distance triathlons. A year of good training without major injuries allowed me to finish the two days of back-to-back racing, but my performances weren't what they used to be. My heart rate stayed well within the 'green zone' for me. The competition had grown much fiercer, but more than that, I couldn't move my legs with the same power and speed as I had before. I believe there was a window of opportunity where the scar tissue in my hand and thigh hadn't quite settled yet right after the accident, so I could move more freely than I can now. While I can go hard over a short distance or slow over a long distance, I find that between my heart and my muscles, the capacity to hold a hard pace for a long time just isn't what it was.

In December 2024, I competed in the Ironman 70.3 Championships in Taupo. Just as at Torremolinos, the competition was far fiercer than

it had been until quite recently. It was an honour to race alongside the new batch of age-group competitors and enjoy the fun of the sport while seeing what is possible for all of us. Racing with them reminded me of what is possible for anyone to achieve, and even as I started slowing down, I was happy to be able to get out there and push the limits with them. During these races, I still felt healthy and strong enough and am proud of my performances even as I adjust to my new condition.

While my doctors have told me that training has added years to my life, I know it has also added life to my years. I don't have to slow down and retire just because I've reached a certain calendar age. I'm not a carton of milk; I won't go bad after a certain date, and neither will any of you. Though I may not be as focused on triathlon as I was while training for the Ironman, I continue to break my week into swim, bike, run, and strength components. I am now looking to master the strength and endurance needed for both racing and living well as I grow older. Recent studies have confirmed that it is a combination of cardiovascular health, muscular strength, and balance and mobility that allows us to live well as we age. I will continue to compete in local triathlons, but I've truly embraced hybrid racing, especially Hyrox, as a new challenge and an opportunity to push myself. My journey with Hyrox began in the summer of 2024, and I vividly remember the struggle with the wall ball event. It took me twenty-nine minutes to finish it due to my leg issue, and it was absolute agony. At that time, I could barely squat and bounce a six-kilogram (thirteen-pound) medicine ball off a target 100 times. I had nothing left at the end of that race, but rather than letting it defeat me, I used it as fuel to improve.

Fast forward to 2025, and I've seen incredible progress. I've not only improved my performance but also achieved podium finishes that I never expected. This year has been a whirlwind of achievements—1st place in the 60-64 AG at the Hyrox Asian Championships in June, alongside a 2nd place finish in the 60-64 Doubles at the same event. I also claimed 1st place in the 60-64 AG at Hyrox Rimini, and 1st place Doubles with Steve Farrell in the 60-69 AG at Hyrox Auckland in February. Even my 4th place finish at Hyrox Brisbane in March was a testament to how far I've come. Something about the sub-threshold nature of Hyrox seems to work well with my new heart condition. Perhaps the details of that journey will be a story for the next book.

These results aren't just about medals; they're about proving to myself that with dedication, smart training, and resilience, I can overcome obstacles like my leg injury and thrive in this new sport. The wall balls that once felt impossible are now just another station to conquer. I've focused on building the strength, mobility, and endurance needed for this type of racing, and it's paid off in ways I couldn't have imagined.

I'm now more determined than ever to keep refining my performance in these races. The challenge of hybrid racing keeps me focused, and it's incredibly rewarding to see measurable improvements over time. I hope my journey inspires all of you to set goals and work toward them, no matter the setbacks. Whether it's in sport or in life, the process of striving, learning, and improving is where the true value lies.

My goals have also expanded to include increasing my responsiveness and support for athletes in numerous places. I have designed and engineered a brand-new shoe with Ortuseight (ortuseight.com), currently selling in Indonesia and Singapore. We have chosen to make this shoe to meet the needs of many athletes, factoring in the financial reality that not everyone can afford pricey shoes from the top brands. We are seeking to replicate the performance of the best carbon-plated, rebound foam shoes for a fraction of the price.

I have also been consulting with SA1NT Layers (saintlayers.cc) to make even more comfortable and effective compression wear. Based on my experiences over the past few years, I have affirmed the benefits of performance clothing both in terms of how I feel on race day and the days that follow hard days—or an accident! Products I helped work on during my time running our sportswear business were definitely effective for improving blood flow to my damaged muscles, but I knew they could be tweaked and improved. I've taken the experience of developing those products and made improvements based on my recent experiences with the more extreme side of recovery. These new products are some of the best that can be found on the market, and I am proud to use them to aid me in running well and feeling good while resting well.

Our strength and resilience become apparent in our capacity to get back up even when it hurts. I know pain intimately from my accidents, the resulting multiple surgeries, and the chronic pain I still suffer in my hand and leg. We can all find a way to live with our pain, and sport has made it easier for me to deal with my injuries. Just as my lifetime of aerobic training has shielded me from some of the effects of my hardening arteries, I am confident that I would be in even greater pain or worse health if I weren't training. The strength and mobility I get from continually using my body and then resting properly keep my joints from wearing out and will let me continue to enjoy the years I have left.

In the end, it is all about finding the right balance that can make you the best version of yourself. We all need to keep using our bodies, wearing them down and letting them heal back stronger. The truth is that all of us are as strong as we let ourselves become. We can recover from just about anything to be physically, mentally, and spiritually stronger than we ever were before. Each of our setbacks is an opportunity to overcome and grow. Even at my age, I am looking to the future and thinking about how I can be the best version of myself for my family, my friends, my clients, and now for you, those who have stuck with me this far as readers. Sports are a testament to resilience, and my life in sport has been one of seeking the best way to build and recover. I wish you the best on your journey and hope that you are inspired to break new personal barriers in strength, durability, and adaptability.

BONUS

Thank you for sticking with us through this journey.

As a bonus, please enjoy any of the six levels of marathon training plans offered by NRG Coaching.

https://www.nrg-coaching.com/

Using the code **"unbreakable"** at check out, you will be able to get 50% off any of the training plans from Level 6 (Beginner; 5–6 hours target) through Level 1 (Advanced; 2:40–3 hours target), valued at £25 GBP (approx $32USD)."

CODE:
unbreakable

Printed in Dunstable, United Kingdom

77995033R00097